Under the Texan Sun

Under the Texan Sun

The Best Recipes from Lone Star Wineries

RHONDA CLOOS

TAYLOR TRADE PUBLISHING
Dallas • Lanham • Boulder • New York • Toronto • Oxford

Copyright © 2005 by Rhonda Cloos
First Taylor Trade Publishing edition 2005

This Taylor Trade Publishing paperback edition of *Under the Texan Sun* is an original publication. It is published by arrangement with the author.

Published by Taylor Trade Publishing
An imprint of The Rowman & Littlefield Publishing Group, Inc.
4501 Forbes Boulevard, Suite 200
Lanham, MD 20706

Distributed by NATIONAL BOOK NETWORK

Library of Congress Cataloging-in-Publication Data

Cloos, Rhonda.
Under the Texan sun : the best recipes from lone star wineries / Rhonda Cloos.
    p.   cm.
Includes index.
ISBN 1-58979-158-4 (pbk. : alk. paper)
1. Cookery.   2. Wineries—Texas.   3. Wine and winemaking—Texas.   I. Title.
TX714.C6377 2005
641.5—dc22   2004020056

♾ ™ The paper used in this publication meets the minimum requirements of American National Standard for Information Sciences—Permanence of Paper for Printed Library Materials, ANSI/NISO Z39.48-1992.

Manufactured in the United States of America.

To
Mark, my partner in wine;
Michael, champion cork thrower; and
Marlee, who stomps grapes with grace and style.

Barbara Gore, my sister,
and her husband Ken and son Ben—
all inspirations for me.

Pamela Cohen, sommelier extraordinaire, cherished
cousin and dear friend.

And to all the great chefs in my family,
past, present, and future.

Contents

Foreword
The Cork in the Road . . . Musings on Food and Wine
Pamela Cohen, Sommelier

There are those serendipitous moments in life that can alter your course forever. Such was the moment in 1987 when the Baroness Philippine de Rothschild brought her wines to my city for a tasting event. When a friend suggested that I volunteer to assist, I jumped at the opportunity, even though my progressive wine experience had only taken me from the unctuous sweet jug wines of my childhood, to the University of Mateus. Who knew that by the end of that day, I would have tasted some of the greatest wines Mouton had produced over the past fifty years.

As luck would have it, the baroness, like a doting mother, stayed to the end to ensure that not a drop went to waste. There were several opened bottles, not yet empty, so she insisted that I pack up the remainders and give them a good home, and this gesture proved to be the proverbial "cork in the road."

Those remaining bottles resulted in the picnic of the decade, where I amazed my friends with great wine and probably the worst refrigerator leftovers those vintages had ever seen. I don't remember the food, but the lineup of brown bags sitting atop a large log at the beach drew a lot of smiles, and, ultimately, the interest of the local mounted police. Thankfully, this meeting resulted only in a brief lecture on the finer points of discretion when bringing wine to the beach. It would be many years again before I tasted any wines that even came close to that magical experience, though it was not for lack of trying. Lack of budget prevented fair comparison, but it did begin an evolutionary process of trying new wines and asking for recommendations. I was particularly puzzled by the fact that, over the years, my increasing knowledge of cooking and enjoying a good restaurant experience was not matched by my still very basic wine knowledge. It frustrated me that I could easily identify foie gras and epoisse on the menu, but the wine list was still a mystery. I didn't really have a clue about wine and food pairing, and any time I hit on the perfect synergy between food and wine, it was wholly by accident. So, I began to read wine magazines, wine books, and wine labels—finally leading to wine classes.

I found an introductory course at a local culinary school, and I was hooked. Even as the only non-industry student in the class, I became as impassioned as the other students who worked with the miracle elixir every day. One evening class led to another, and finally, the decision to become a sommelier led to a leave of absence from my bureaucratic career to attend full-day classes for six months to earn my diploma. I was not only the sole non-industry student in the class, but the oldest. My young compatriots took me under wing when it came time to learn to properly open and decant an old port, or pull the cork on a bottle of champagne with only a mere whisper. I, in turn, took charge of ensuring that my small study group, formed on day one, maintained its pace each week. It was a grueling schedule of taking notes and leading discussions at our twice-weekly blind tastings, hosted on a rotating basis at one of our homes, coupled with endless chatter about such things as the differences between the soil types of Burgundy and the Rhone Valley.

We nervously prepared for our sommelier exams, comprised of essays, multiple-choice questions, food and wine pairing, service expertise, and the all too intimidating blind tasting. Over a period of two full days, we defended our individual wine and food pairings to an ever-questioning adjudicator. We decanted and served, sniffed, swirled, tasted, and provided detailed notes on our tasting results; wrote essays on wine regions many of us had yet to visit; and answered seemingly endless questions about unpronounceable wine varieties in obscure regions of the world. I wondered, more than once, why I would put myself through such a process. While the answer has revealed itself to me on many occasions since, I had managed to run on adrenaline for the weeks leading up to the exam. Sleep didn't seem to be an option. I was standing over my kitchen sink at 4 a.m. the morning of the tasting portion of the exam, comparing wines that had been challenging me for the past six months. Taste . . . spit . . . taste . . . spit (spitting becomes a ritualistic habit and second nature when tasting a number of wines, though not to be repeated in restaurants).

The work paid off, and while my exam results were rewarding, nothing could have prepared me for the unanticipated doors that have opened. That "cork in the road" has led to concurrent endeavors in teaching wine courses for the International Sommelier Guild, tour guiding through the world's wine regions, becoming a director of my local wine club, organizing and pouring at wine tasting events, judging sommelier exams, and occasionally working at my favorite wine store. I mention this only to illustrate the diversity of possibilities within the industry, and to emphatically refuse to ever accept the notion that I'm an "expert" when it comes to wine. I am a perpetual student and appreciative amateur who readily recognizes how little I truly know about a vast and diverse subject.

Nevertheless, it's fun, and best of all, a glass of wine shared among friends is one of the best feelings in the world.

I would encourage you to experiment as you read this book. Look at the suggested pairings and recipes offered by those who have taken the time to match their wines to the regional cuisine of Texas—or match their cuisine to the wines of Texas!

There are many wonderful books on the subject of food and wine pairing. My personal heroes and "experts" include Jancis Robinson, Andrea Immer, and Joanna Simons. Each has much to offer, but keep in mind that no one but you has your palate and taste sensibility. So, I'll offer some simple suggestions that may help you on your way, but the rest of the journey is up to you.

You've probably heard the saying, "reds with meat, whites with fish." That's a fair guideline in some cases, but it's just a guideline. Strong, tannic reds are often paired with steak for good reason. The proteins in steak counteract the tannins in the wine. Tannins are those components that leave the mouth-drying sensation you may experience when drinking strong tea. The resulting effect is that both the flavors of the steak and the wine are enhanced. Both tend to appear "smooth."

Does that mean that white wine would not pair well with meat? Not at all. First, we're talking about a matter of personal taste. A number of full-bodied white wines work well with meats. In particular, pork is a good match for many whites, and I'm sure you'll get some recommendations from the Texas wine producers about matching whites to some extraordinary dishes. Fleshy, "meaty" fish are equally well matched with some lighter-bodied reds.

A key point to keep in mind is that a sommelier making wine and food pairing suggestions will take into consideration the "texture" of the wine with that of the food. So, if you are eating meat, or even fish, with a rich, velvety, butter-based sauce, the recommendation may be for a full-bodied white wine, because the "textures" match. On the other hand, if you're eating such a rich food, it might also be appropriate to make a recommendation that contrasts with the richness of that texture. So a wine with high acidity would be used to cleanse the palate, and counteract the mouth-coating richness found in the sauce. The wine could be red or white. Its role, however, is both to refresh and quench the palate.

Acidity in wine causes a mouthwatering sensation, which has the opposite of the effect of tannin on the palate. This character is found in many red and white wines, although the tannin effect is only found in reds. Simply prepared seafoods are a wonderful match with high-acid whites. Once you start layering on various types of sauces, though, sommeliers will pay more attention to the predominant flavors in that main dish, which may be the sauce. Aromatic Asian-based spices will match well with aromatic white wines, whereas warm, baking-spice flavors would favor reds.

Alcohol affects how the palate reacts to both food and wine as well. If you are drinking a wine that is relatively high in alcohol (13 percent or more), you'll find that spicy foods will taste hotter. Not only that, but the perception on your palate will also make the wine seem "hot." That's something to keep in mind when taking on some of those Texas specialties. Whether it's chili or barbecue, if you're drinking wine, look for something with lower alcohol, so that you can taste both the wine and the food!

Salt can have an effect on wine flavor too. Big red wines tend to taste "tinny" when drunk while eating particularly salty foods. If you like salt, or your dish is flavored with a sauce that has a high component of sodium, such as soy or teriyaki, select a wine that's low in those gum-gripping tannins.

As for dessert, be sure to leave room for something sweet! I love the Aussies with their knack for coming up with interesting descriptors. They refer to their sweet wines as "stickies"! Of course, Texas is known for its fortified wines made in the style of port. The warm caramel and nutty flavors meld well with similar desserts. I'm sure you'll be able to come up with any number of mouthwatering combinations. One simple observance, to optimize your meal-ending epiphany, is to try to ensure that the wine is sweeter than the dessert. Going in the other direction makes both the wine and the dessert taste flat. However, if this is not possible, the sensible solution is to treat them both as separate courses. It's a great way to sneak in two desserts and pace yourself in the process!

Always remember to raise a glass to absent friends, because every great wine experience is only enhanced by sharing, even if it's from a distance—enjoy!

Pamela Cohen lives in Vancouver, British Columbia, and is a sommelier and member of the International Sommelier

Guild, the Society of Wine Educators, the Vancouver American Wine Society, and the Vancouver chapter of Les Chevaliers des Vins de France. She and the author are cousins and good friends who have shared many childhood adventures that led to the paths they have chosen today.

Acknowledgments

Recipes have guided me since childhood. Some people simply wing it in the kitchen. I do best if I start with a recipe and add my own personal touch. When I applied for my first job in the food industry, my resume captured attention because I made myself into a recipe ("blend a college education with a passion for hard work," you get the gist).

While writing this book, I also used a recipe, blending these ingredients: a passion for food and wine; outstanding Texas wineries; the advice of my sommelier cousin; the assistance of great Texas chefs; a supportive circle of friends; and the help of my family, who didn't mind going without meals while their personal chef was tethered to the computer. I blended the ingredients and jumped headfirst into the sauté pan. Writing a book is intense.

This book could not have been written without the help of many individuals. I am going to try to recognize each one. My sincere apologies if I left someone out.

I offer sincere appreciation to Ginnie Bivona, my initial editor, and to Rick Rinehart, Mandy Phillips, and Jehanne Schweitzer from Taylor Trade. Thank you.

Tamra Andrews helped shape the idea for *Under the Texan Sun* one Saturday morning as we drank coffee at her kitchen table. Margaret and Frank Krasovec provided contact names during early research. Sherrie Frachtman kept me supplied with her fresh and innovative ideas; many came to fruition on these pages. Susan Whitman helped search for recipes and listened to hundreds of miles of wine and food talk. She also took on the role of photographer, with special assistance from Bill. Dana Joslin and Frank Federer graciously offered assistance in collecting recipes from chefs. Cathy Smith provided excused absences from bowling. Melissa Greenwell offered recipe suggestions. Award-winning novelist Sarah Bird answered my frantic questions covering various aspects of churning out a book. Ellen Garbsch provided daily e-mails from afar, offering her support and encouragement. Sebastian Garbsch calmed my spirit through his photographs, which adorn my office walls. John and Lucinda Roenigk provided wine information and industry contact names. Amos and Lynn Salvador supplied reading materials regarding the art and science of wine. Martha Dorward offered friendship and laughter as I wrote. Steve and Kathy Salm provided wine education (and some gourmet meals) back in those California days. Maureen Thacker, who developed recipes for a living at one point in her life, offered her culinary assistance and shared recipes.

My dear sister Barbara Gore provided recipe ideas, reading materials, and constant support throughout the project. Her husband Ken served fine wines during my visits to their home. And my nephew Ben gave me a healthy dose of distraction during the final writing stages by helping his team have a winning football season. My late mother provided the inspiration to bake and cook from scratch, and my dad gave me that writing gene.

The wineries of Texas graciously shared their histories and their recipes with me. I have come to appreciate that owning a winery is a labor of love, and I sincerely appreciate every moment these individuals spent educating me on the Texas wine industry. They answered questions and provided wine labels for the artwork in this book. I'd like to specifically recognize Karen Johnson, Alamosa; Nicole Bendele, Becker; Bob and Evelyn Oberhelman, Bell Mountain; Patrick Johnson, Blue Mountain; Steve Wilson and Kim McPherson, Cap*Rock; Paula K. Williamson, Chisholm Trail; Jerry Delaney and Bénédicte Rhyne, Delaney; Gary, Kathy, and Laura Elliot, Driftwood; Bonnie Houser, Dry Comal Creek; Ed and Susan Auler, Fall Creek; Rick and Madelyn Naber, Flat Creek; Troy and Carolyn Rose, Grape Creek; Gladys Haak, Haak; Gina Puente-Brancato and Margie Knight, La Bodega; Camille McBee, La Buena Vida; Caris Turpen, LightCatcher; Russell Gillentine, Llano Estacado; Maureen McReynolds, McReynolds; Paul and Merrill Bonarrigo, Messina Hof; Margaret McMillan, Pheasant Ridge; Gill and Peggy Bledsoe, Pillar Bluff; Bob and Jeanne Cottle and their friend David Vucovic, Pleasant Hill; Danny Hernandez and Annette Mainz, Sister Creek; Madeleine Manigold, Spicewood; Nancy Haehnel and Bénédicte Rhyne, Ste. Genevieve; Kathy Gilstrap, Texas Hills; Alton and Lana Gates, Wichita Falls; and Brian Wilgus, Woodrose. To each of you, I offer heartfelt thanks and wish you the best of everything. May your grapes flourish!

A number of chefs graciously agreed to share recipes from their personal collections and cookbooks they have authored. Thank you to Chef Jeff Blank and Shanny Lott, Hudson's on the Bend; Chef De Andra Breeden, Fresh Chef; Chef David J.

Bull, The Driskill Hotel; Chef Shawn Cirkiel, Cirkiel Catering, Inc. (and thanks to Marty Cirkiel); Chef Terry Conlan, Lake Austin Spa Resort; Chef Sam Dickey, The Granite Café; Jane King, Central Market Foodie; and Chef Roger Mollet, Fonds de Cuisine.

Texas is home to a fabulous source for freshly made cheeses, the Mozzarella Company in Dallas. Special thanks to its owner and founder, Paula Lambert, who shared two recipes from her book, *The Cheese Lover's Cookbook & Guide.*

Another fine company in Texas is the New York, Texas, Cheesecake Company in Athens. Its owners, Bud and Nancy Hicks, provided information and support as I wrote both of my books. (And their cheesecake sure pairs well with that Muscat Canelli.)

Bénédicte Rhyne, her husband Richy, and their family welcomed us into their home and provided outstanding French cuisine, delightful Texas wines, and stimulating conversation, as well as their treasured friendship. Bénédicte answered many questions for me and agreed to share her thoughts on wine and food pairings through an interview in this book.

I can never say thank-you enough to a very special family member who provided support, encouragement, knowledge, and friendship from day one. I owe a huge debt of gratitude to my cousin Pamela Cohen, who is a sommelier, dear friend, and talented writer and musician. Pam promptly answered every technical wine question that arose (and believe me, there were many), with humor and a sense of good cheer. She is a fine teacher, and I am very fortunate to have known her all my life. Pam wrote the foreword for this book.

I raise a glass of Cabernet to the memory of my friend, fellow author, and mentor, Chuck Meyer, who really wanted to see this book.

Last but not least, my husband Mark and our children, Michael and Marlee, offered inspiration. They taught me that looking at the stars out in back, watching cartwheels in the living room, or tossing a football in the front yard calms the spirit and stimulates the mind, especially in the final stages of writing a book. They willingly spent precious vacation time accompanying me on wine tours around the state, serving as chauffeur, photographers, fellow grape pickers and stompers, and most of all cherished traveling companions. Thank you, Mark, Michael, and Marlee. I promise to feed you well.

How to Use This Book

Under the Texan Sun is first and foremost a cookbook. You'll find recipes that contain Texas wines or pair nicely with them. Most of the recipes are from Texas wineries; there is also a chapter on wine recipes developed by Texas chefs, one on wine and cheese, and another that addresses the challenge of pairing wine with chocolate. I've also included a collection of recipes from my personal files.

The book can be read from cover to cover like a novel, or you can pick it up and read the sections that interest you at the moment. I suggest three ways to use this book:

1. *Try the recipes.* This book is filled with innovative recipes that contain wine or pair well with wine. Experiment with the recipes in your own kitchen. Prepare them for a family dinner or your next dinner party. The recipes are written in a format that is easy to follow. Give 'em a whirl, and be sure to serve a Texas wine as an accompaniment. Most recipes include wine and food pairings to remove the guesswork.

2. *Discover Texas wineries.* Read about the wineries, and meet the people who work hard, sometimes overcoming challenging conditions, to bring you some of the best wines available. Learn about the architecture of the wineries, the types of grapes they grow, and why the vintner selected a particular location. I hope the information about the wineries and the vintners will further your enjoyment of the recipes.

3. *Visit the wineries.* This book contains brief information covering the hours of operation. Before you go, it's wise to check the wineries' websites (they have wonderful maps!) to make sure the hours have not changed.

Note that "Selected Wines" are listed for each winery. This is a partial wine list.

Welcome to the adventure of cooking with Texas wines. May you enjoy preparing these recipes and feasting on the fruits of your labor.

Lone appétit!

Introduction
Under the Texan Sun

The year was 1979. My husband Mark and I lived in Los Angeles, where he was a graduate student in geology and I was a food service manager. While I churned out a few thousand portions of cafeteria meals each day, Mark focused on how the Coast Ranges of California formed over the eons of time.

Every so often, the northern California hillsides called out to Mark. He'd pack the sledgehammer into the car and trek up north for a weekend of fieldwork. I tagged along on many occasions, happy to leave the L.A. smog even for a few days.

It didn't take long before I took note of a major bonus. Not only were the hillsides alive with geology, something else was going on there.

Grapevines. They seemed to be growing everywhere, carpeting the slopes like heather in Scotland. California had a new attraction besides Disneyland. This time, the California Gold Rush was the quest for Chardonnay!

As luck would have it, portions of Mark's field area were smack in the middle of the wine-growing region. Back then, the Napa Valley seemed like new, uncharted land. The expensive wine tours and trendy restaurants hadn't yet arrived. In geologic terms, it was the Jurassic phase of the California wine industry. Tastings and tours were free of charge and free of crowds.

I was overwhelmed the first time I set foot in a winery. The tour guide enthusiastically explained why grapes grow in California because of the region's climatic conditions, and how the skins are left on the red grapes during fermentation and removed to make whites.

Cool cavernous cellars stacked with wooden barrels transported me to a place where all my senses responded, as if on cue. The aroma of the fermenting grapes, the chill in the air, and thick stone cellar walls left me in awe of the emerging California wine industry. The tasting rooms offered the final touch, the ooh-la-la of the tour. There, complimentary wines were served at the perfect temperature, in clear crystal stemware. Starting with the whites and moving along to the full-bodied reds, we swirled glasses and sipped the delightful California wines.

We were very disciplined on those trips. After all, Mark had a thesis to finish. It was work before play, geology before wine. Mark roamed around the hills collecting small chunks of the California landscape while I read or helped him stuff rocks into canvas bags. When we closed the last sample bag of the day, we'd follow the yellow brick road to our own Emerald City, the nearest winery.

At that time, California wines were still trying to gain a toehold over the imports. Mark and I immediately liked the idea of supporting a growing, local industry.

We'd return from our weekend geology/wine jaunts with a trunkload of rocks for his thesis and wine for our parties. On special occasions, we held tastings where French and California wines stood beside one another, their labels carefully concealed under brown paper bags. Guests were instructed to take a taste and guess which was which. (To illustrate our lack of knowledge, I'm not even sure that we actually compared the same varietals.)

In 1981, Mark finished his thesis and our Napa Valley wine tours came to an abrupt halt. It was okay, for I was ready to leave California for more stable ground. We headed east to Texas, leaving the California grape industry to become bigger than we would ever imagine.

I had lived in the Lone Star State for two years before, in 1983, I had my first encounter with a Texas wine. (That just happens to be the same year that the Texas Department of Agriculture became involved in the state's wine industry.) Mark and I were at the party of the century, a gala celebrating the hundredth anniversary of the University of Texas. Each guest was sent home from the gala with two bottles of wine, one white and one red. Not just any wine—these bottles were Texas High Plains, with a personalized University of Texas label stuck on the front. Those two bottles still occupy a place in our Texas souvenir collection.

Following the gala, nearly a decade passed before I began to notice Texas wines becoming more prominent on store shelves. I bought them, eager once again to support a young local industry. By the end of the twentieth century, Texas wines were more than just a few bottles on the shelf. To me, they had reached the stage where Napa Valley had been a few decades ago. These days, acres of Texas hillsides are becoming carpeted with grapevines, just like another place a few thousand miles to the west.

Today, Texas has seven viticultural areas, and the Texas

Hill Country is the second largest wine-growing region in the United States. Over the years, our personal wine rack has grown to reflect the trend; most of the slots are filled with wines from Lone Star vintners.

Extraordinary award-winning wines are produced in Texas. The industry is flowing with entrepreneurial energy and creative spirit. Texas laws have pulled off the cork, freeing wineries to serve and sell their wines, even in dry counties. And mail order within the state is possible as well. Visit a winery and experience firsthand the pride that the vintners pour into their hard work. Texas wineries are going places, and now is the time to hop on the bandwagon and enjoy them.

In 2002 my first book, *Texas Food Companies: A Tasty Guide*—a compilation of facts and trivia covering the Texas food industry—was published. With a food book under my belt, the next logical step was one on food and wine. Thinking back to those early Napa Valley experiences, I recalled touring my first winery, where the casks were hand carved and the vintner's family had put together a cookbook of their favorite recipes. In my mind, this book on recipes from Texas wineries had taken shape.

I was drawn to the concept of transporting readers into the heart and soul of the wineries. Fine wines require proper microclimate, drainage, and soil. But the human factor is key. Premium people make premium wines. On these pages, you'll learn about the people behind Texas wineries, why they do what they do, and how their personalities are reflected in their vineyards, their wineries, and ultimately in their wines. They share their stories and personal recipes. I encourage you to bring their wines into your own kitchen.

A final word on wine and food. The pair brings to mind one of my favorite songs, Frank Sinatra's "Love and marriage" ("go together like a horse and carriage"). Wine and food do go together like a horse and carriage, but the ride will be bumpy and you might not get where you want to go if you don't pay attention to the details. The recipes on these pages use top quality ingredients—both food and wine—in the preparation of meals that feature both flavor and flair.

Under the Texan sun, grapes bask by day, developing the character and complexity reflected in the wines of the Lone Star State. Cook with pride; flavor your next meal with the reds and whites of Texas.

Alamosa Wine Cellars

Bend, Texas

If you go . . .
Alamosa Wine Cellars
677 CR 430
P.O. Box 212
Bend, TX 76824
Phone: (325) 628-3313
Website:
www.alamosawinecellars.com
Hours:
Open first weekend of every month,
Hill Country Wine Trail weekends,
and these holiday weekends:
Memorial Day, Labor Day, July 4th,
and Thanksgiving weekend.
Otherwise, call for appointment.
Check website, as the winery is open
for some holidays.

Selected Wines
Sangiovese
Sangiovese Reserva
Syrah
Palette (Rhone Blend)
"El Guapo" Tempranillo
Viognier
Jacque Lapin ("Jack Rabbit" in
French, a dry Chenin Blanc)
Mataro (The first varietal Mourvedre
made by Alamosa; Mataro is the
Italian version.)

Alamosa Wine Cellars sits at an elevation of 1,200 feet in the northernmost tip of the Texas Hill Country. Here the microclimate and proximity to the Colorado River offer optimum grape-growing conditions.

In 1996, with the help of family and friends, owners Jim and Karen Johnson planted Alamosa's first grapes on five acres. The Johnsons initially focused on Viognier and Sangiovese varieties, with a few rows of Cabernet Sauvignon and Ruby Cabernet. The following year they planted another two-and-a-half acres, and in 1998 they reached ten acres of plants with the addition of Syrah, Mourvedre, and Malvasia Bianca. Today, the winery continues to operate as a team effort, with family and friends chipping in to help.

Alamosa's winemaking philosophy stems from a belief that blending grapes results in the most desirable wines. Blends are made in the field or during the fermentation process. The Johnsons take great care in maintaining their vineyard to produce well-cared-for grapes that are at the forefront of their wines.

The hard work has yielded good results, and the Johnsons produce a number of award-winning wines. In addition to retail stores, Alamosa wines are featured on the menus of many fine restaurants throughout Texas.

When Jim Johnson opened Alamosa, he was already an experienced winemaker. After studying oenology at the University of California at Davis, he was a winemaker for several distinguished California wineries. When he returned to Texas, he worked for a few neighboring Hill Country wineries before devoting himself to Alamosa full-time in 1998.

Karen Johnson plays an active role at Alamosa, working with sales and marketing, and serving as "harvest crew boss." She and Jim opened Alamosa to the public in 1999. Over the years, Karen and Jim have become active members of the Texas wine industry, and the couple is featured at a number of state-wide wine events. They also teach a variety of wine and food classes. One exciting event is a wine enthusiasts' cruise to Cozumel led by the Johnsons and the Gilstraps (from Texas Hills Vineyard).

Jim and Karen share several favorite recipes; each carries a personal story reflecting their experiences.

 ## Braised Rabbit

Serves 4

Jim and I traveled to Italy in 1998 with Gary and Kathy Gilstrap of Texas Hills Vineyard. We visited the Tuscan wineries and loved the wine and food. One day at lunch we ate at a small trattoria in San Donato where we had rabbit stew with the traditional spinach and white beans. Several months later, after I had tried to duplicate this wonderful Tuscan meal, Jim suggested I use my osso buco recipe and substitute rabbit for the veal. It was really close! Serve this up with some cannellini beans, steamed spinach, Italian bread, and fragrant olive oil. And, the Alamosa Sangiovese, of course.—Karen Johnson

> 1 cup onion, chopped
> ²/₃ cup carrot, finely chopped
> ²/₃ cup celery, finely chopped
> 4 tablespoons butter
> 2 cloves garlic
> 2 strips lemon peel
> ¹/₃ cup vegetable oil
> 2 rabbits, cut up (Central Market has rabbit.)
> Flour, for dredging

1 cup dry white wine

1 cup good-quality beef broth

1½ cups canned imported Italian plum tomatoes, coarsely chopped, with juice

½ teaspoon fresh thyme

2 bay leaves

2 or 3 sprigs parsley

Freshly ground black pepper

Salt

1. Preheat oven to 350°F.

2. Finely chop all vegetables.

3. Place butter in a heavy-bottomed pot (one that is large enough to hold the rabbit pieces in one layer and can be placed in the oven). Melt butter. Add onion, carrots, and celery.

4. Cook 6 to 7 minutes, then add the garlic and lemon peel. Cook another 2 to 3 minutes until the vegetables soften and wilt. Remove from heat. Set aside.

5. Place vegetable oil in a skillet. When the oil is quite hot, add the flour-dredged rabbit pieces. (Do not flour the rabbit until just before adding to oil, and shake off excess flour).

6. Cook the rabbit pieces, turning to brown on all sides. Place the browned rabbit onto the vegetables in the large ovenproof pot.

7. Pour off nearly all the frying oil and add the wine to the skillet. Reduce it over medium heat while scraping up the browned bits from the bottom of the pan.

8. Pour the skillet juices over the rabbit in the pot.

9. Add broth to the skillet, bring it to a simmer, and add it to the pot. Add the tomatoes with their juice, bay leaves,

thyme, parsley, salt, and pepper to the rabbit pot. The broth should nearly cover the rabbit pieces. If not, add more broth. Bring the contents of the pot to a simmer.

10. Cover tightly, and place the pot in the lower third of the oven. Cook for about 1 hour—until the meat is tender when prodded with a fork, and a dense, creamy sauce has formed. Turn the pieces and baste every 20 minutes. Add a few tablespoons of water if the broth gets reduced too much.

11. When the rabbit is done, transfer to a warm platter and pour the sauce over the pieces. If the sauce is too thin, reduce it over medium-high heat.

Serving Suggestion: The Tuscans prepare white beans as the traditional side dish. Polenta would be a good substitute.

Wine: Serve with Alamosa Sangiovese.

Note: Karen Johnson adapted the recipe from a basic osso buco recipe that appeared in *Essentials of Classic Italian Cooking,* by Marcella Hazan (Knopf, 1992). She suggests increasing the cooking time to a total of 2 hours, checking after 1 hour if veal is used.

 ## Beef Tenderloin Canapés with Horseradish Sauce

Serves 4–8, depending on size of tenderloin

This is a great "heavy hors d'oeuvre" for a wine tasting party. It stands up to the bigger wines.—Karen Johnson

1 whole or half beef tenderloin
Herbes de Provence, or cracked black pepper
Salt, to taste
Garlic powder, to taste
Easy Horseradish Sauce (recipe follows)
About 2 loaves of coarse, seeded bread, sliced thin
Watercress or other fresh herb

1. Preheat oven to 400°F.
2. Roll beef tenderloin in herbes de Provence (or cracked pepper), salt, and garlic powder.
3. Roast in preheated oven for about 10 minutes. Reduce heat to 350°F and roast to an internal temperature of 140°F or more for desired doneness. This can be done a day ahead. Chill the beef and slice thinly.
4. Using a fluted cutter, cut small circles out of the bread slices. Place a folded slice of beef on a circle and top with a dollop of horseradish sauce. Garnish with a leaf of watercress or other fresh herb.

Easy Horseradish Sauce:

1. Mix equal amounts of mayonnaise and sour cream.
2. Add horseradish, lemon juice, and salt and pepper to taste.

Variation: Add orange zest to the sauce (Karen Johnson's favorite way to serve it).
Wine: Serve with Alamosa Palette or El Guapo.

Classic Provençal Tapanade

Makes about 1 cup of spread

This is a great appetizer and easy to do. Keep the ingredients on hand and serve it to unexpected guests or for impromptu wine gatherings.—Karen Johnson

1 cup kalamata or other dark, pitted, brine-cured olives
2 cloves garlic, coarsely chopped
1 tablespoon anchovy paste, or 3–4 canned anchovies
Black pepper
Juice from about ½ of a medium lemon
Olive oil, good quality, fragrant

1. Place olives, garlic, and anchovy paste in food processor. Pulse until mixture achieves coarse, grainy consistency. Add black pepper and lemon juice. Pulse again.
2. Add the olive oil in a slow stream while pulsing. Do not overprocess to a paste.

Serving Suggestion: Serve with pita toasts, crackers, or crostini.

Karen Johnson's Crostini:

1. Brush sliced baguettes with olive oil on one side.
2. Toast in the oven on a cookie sheet, and then turn and toast the other side.
3. Rub the olive oil side with a peeled clove of garlic. These are delicious eaten by themselves.

Quick Krab Nibbles

Serves 8-10 (appetizer-sized servings)

Karen Johnson says guests think she worked for hours to prepare this, but it is really a "quick crowd pleaser."

One 8-ounce container prepared Krab spread (see Note)
6 English muffins, split

1. Spread each English muffin half with about one heaping tablespoon Krab spread.
2. Place in oven and broil until the spread is bubbly.
3. Cut into quarters and serve hot.

Note: Randalls makes a good Krab spread, but most supermarkets have their own version. Alternatively, you can make a real crab spread with cheese and spices.
Wine: Serve with Alamosa Viognier.

 ## Shrimp in Garlic Sauce

Serves 4 as a fish course, 6 as an appetizer

This is Karen Johnson's favorite tapa.

$^1/_2$ to $^3/_4$ pound small, Gulf Coast shrimp, shelled and
    deveined, tail left on
Coarse salt
8 tablespoons good-quality olive oil
3 large cloves garlic, peeled and very coarsely chopped
1 dried red chili pepper, stem and seeds removed, torn into
    two pieces

$^1/_2$ teaspoon paprika, preferably Spanish style
1 tablespoon minced parsley
1 loaf French or Italian bread, for dipping

1. Dry the shrimp and sprinkle with the salt on both sides. Let stand 10 minutes.
2. Heat oil on top of stove in an 8-inch casserole, preferably earthenware.
3. Add the garlic and chili pepper. When the garlic begins to turn golden, add shrimp. Cook over medium-high heat, stirring for about 2 minutes or until the shrimp is just done. Be careful not to overcook or the shrimp will be tough.
4. Sprinkle with parsley, paprika, and additional salt to taste.
5. Serve immediately, right in the cooking dish, and provide lots of good bread for dipping in the oil.

Wine: Although white wines are generally served with shrimp, try Alamosa Grenache or El Guapo with this flavorful, garlicky dish.

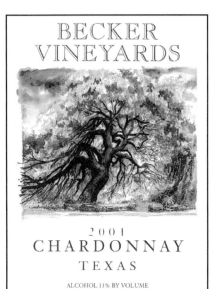

2

Becker Vineyards
Stonewall, Texas

If you go . . .
Becker Vineyards
P.O. Box 393
Stonewall, TX 78671
Phone: (830) 644-2681
Website: www.beckervineyards.com
Hours:
Monday–Thursday: 10 a.m.–5 p.m.
Friday and Saturday: 10 a.m.–6 p.m.
Sunday: Noon–6 p.m.

Selected Wines
Fumé Blanc Estate Bottled
Chardonnay
Chenin Blanc
Viognier
Provencal (Cabernet Sauvignon,
    Sauvignon Blanc blend)
Merlot
Claret
Cabernet Sauvignon Reserve
Cabernet-Syrah
Zinfandel
Gewürztraminer
Muscat Canelli
Vintage Port Estate Bottled

Richard and Bunny Becker established Becker Vineyards in 1992, and enjoyed their first harvest three years later. Today, the winery's reputation for award-winning wines extends well beyond its Hill Country roots. The winery was featured in the November 30, 2002, issue of *Wine Spectator,* and in July 2003, Becker Vineyards wines were served to the president of Spain.

The vineyard now includes forty-six acres, planted with the help of Armon Grantham and Jim Brown, general manager. Grape varieties grown in the vineyard include Viognier, Grenache, Mourvedre, Syrah, Chardonnay, Sauvignon Blanc, Malbec, Petite Verdot, Cabernet Sauvignon, Cabernet Franc, and Merlot.

Becker Vineyards has seen several expansions since its early years. The tasting room opened in 1996, featuring a nineteenth-century bar that originally stood in the Green Tree Saloon in San Antonio.

In 1998, Bunny and Richard added a touch of France to the vineyard when they planted three acres of fragrant lavender after a visit to Provence. An assortment of lavender products is available in the gift shop. A lavender festival, held in June, features lavender products for sale, demonstrations, live music, a lavender luncheon, and wine tastings and tours.

Adjacent to the winery is a log cabin dating back to 1890. There, guests are accommodated in the Homestead Bed and Breakfast. The rental fee includes use of the cabin, a bottle of wine, and a delicious selection of baked goods at breakfast.

A reception hall, the Lavender Haus, features a replica of the historic barn at the LBJ settlement in Johnson City, Texas. The hall is used for events such as winery dinners, conferences, weddings, and other vineyard gatherings.

The staff at Becker Vineyards shares two dessert recipes featuring their award-winning wines.

Port Pecans

Makes 8-10 topping-sized servings (makes 2 cups topping)

Public relations coordinator Nichole Bendele shares this recipe, which was originally developed by former employee Paul Gingrich.

1 cup pecan halves
$^1/_2$ cup sugar
$^1/_4$ cup Becker Vintage Port

1. Combine sugar and Port in pan over high heat. Stir constantly. As soon as mixture begins to boil, add pecans. Stir and turn pecans to prevent burning. Within 5 to 6 minutes, mixture becomes thick, and Port red color changes to a dark caramel color. Remove from heat at this point. *Do not touch pecans*—mixture is very hot.
2. Carefully—without touching by hand—spread pecans on cookie sheet. Let cool 15–20 minutes.
3. Break into small pieces when cool.

Serving Suggestion: Munch on the Port Pecans as a snack, crumble on top of ice cream, add to the top of a chocolate cake or cheesecake, or crumble onto a warm Brie wedge.

Port Brownies

Makes 1 recipe of brownie mix

Public relations coordinator Nichole Bendele often hears suggestions from Becker Vineyards patrons. Several customers have offered this delicious brownie variation using their Port.

One box of your favorite brownie mix
Becker Vintage Port

1. Follow directions on brownie mix, substituting Port for the water.
2. Bake as directed, and cut into squares.

3

Bell Mountain Vineyards
Fredericksburg, Texas

If you go . . .
Bell Mountain Vineyards
1463 Bell Mountain Road
P.O. Box 756
Fredericksburg, TX 78624
Phone: (830) 685-3297
Website: www.bellmountainwine.com
Hours:
Saturday: 10 a.m.–5 p.m.
Other times by appointment.

Selected Wines
Chardonnay
Dry Riesling
Late Harvest Riesling
Cabernet Sauvignon
Merlot
Pinot Noir

If you go . . .
Oberhof
1406 S. U.S. Highway 87
Fredericksburg, TX 78624
Phone: (830) 997-0124
Website: www.bellmountainwine.com
Hours:
Monday–Saturday: 10 a.m.–6 p.m.
Sunday: Noon–6 p.m.

Selected Wines
Berry Light Wine with Natural
    Flavors
Liebchen Classic White Wine
Mead Texas Wildflower Honey Wine
Blush Light Wine
KrisKrindel Red Wine with Natural
    Spices and Flavors
Peach Light Wine with Natural Flavor

Named for a geologic formation designated by the U.S. Geological Survey in 1885, Bell Mountain Vineyards sits nearly two thousand feet above sea level. Owners Bob and Evelyn Oberhelman offer a wide variety of wines and events at their chateau-style winery. Bell Mountain wines are estate bottled, meaning they are produced from grapes grown on the owners' vineyard.

In addition to Bell Mountain wines, the Oberhelmans produce Oberhof Wines, which include specialties such as Blush and Peach, and some sparkling varieties described as "light wines with natural flavors." The Oberhelmans welcome guests at both Bell Mountain Vineyards, located in the countryside north of Fredericksburg, and at Oberhof, which is just south of Main Street in Fredericksburg.

Visitors to Bell Mountain Vineyards enjoy winery tours, tastings, and a gift shop featuring wines and gourmet food products. Those who visit Oberhof may view a video describing the grape-growing process and winemaking at Bell Mountain, followed by tastings on the pleasant outdoor deck and a chance to shop for wines and gourmet foods.

Bell Mountain Vineyards is home to a number of special events. During the "Holidays at the Vineyards," beginning in late November and extending into December, guests bring picnic baskets and sip KrisKrindel (Oberhof's hot spiced red wine) while listening to festive holiday tunes. The Oberhelmans encourage visitors to stop by throughout the year. Their website proclaims, "Every Saturday is a festive day at Bell Mountain Vineyards."

Bob and Evelyn Oberhelman share this recipe for marinated beef tenderloin.

Bell Mountain Roast Beef of Tenderloin

Serves 6-8

Robert P. Oberhelman, wine master and president of Bell Mountain Vineyards, provided this delicious recipe, which combines beef tenderloin with Bell Mountain Cabernet Sauvignon.

3-5 pound beef tenderloin, excess fat and tip end removed

For Marinade:

Bell Mountain Cabernet Sauvignon, enough to cover the
   roast
3 shallot bulbs, peeled and chopped
2 tablespoons fresh thyme leaves, removed from stems but
   not chopped
1/4 of a fresh lemon, chopped (peel included)

1. Marinate beef in refrigerator for 16-24 hours in a narrow, deep glass casserole dish.
2. Turn roast every 6-8 hours.
3. After marinating beef, drain marinade from casserole dish into saucepan and reserve.

For Roast:

Softened butter
Coarse black pepper
Sea salt

1. Preheat oven to 500°F while preparing beef for roasting.
2. Place tenderloin into baking casserole dish that has been greased with butter or sprayed with nonstick cooking spray.

3. Spread softened butter over top of tenderloin and pat on the following from the marinade: fresh thyme leaves, shallot bulbs, and lemon.

4. Sprinkle top of tenderloin with coarse black pepper and sea salt.

5. Place tenderloin in preheated oven. Sear tenderloin in casserole dish for 5 minutes per pound.

6. Reduce heat to 225°F and bake 20–30 minutes per pound, depending on desired degree of doneness.

For Sauce:

Wine drained from marinade (see Note)
4 tablespoons butter
2 tablespoons flour
For Garnish: Parsley

1. Heat wine in saucepan to boiling, and reduce by one-half. Blend the 4 tablespoons butter into 2 tablespoons flour. Stir into marinade. Continue to stir constantly until sauce thickens.

2. Garnish serving platter with parsley.

3. Carve tenderloin into half-inch slices and arrange on platter.

Note: Some people are averse to reusing a marinade, even if boiled. An alternative is to use a fresh amount of Bell Mountain Cabernet Sauvignon for the sauce.

Wine: Serve with latest vintage Bell Mountain Cabernet Sauvignon.

4

BLUE MOUNTAIN WINES
1999
ESTATE

Cabernet Sauvignon

Texas Davis Mountains

PRODUCED AND BOTTLED BY
BLUE MOUNTAIN VINEYARD, INC. • FORT DAVIS, TEXAS
BWTX85

Alcohol 13.5% By Volume

Blue Mountain Vineyard & Winery

Fort Davis, Texas

If you go . . .
Blue Mountain Vineyard & Winery

HCR 74, Box 7
Fort Davis, TX 79734
Phone/Fax: (915) 426-3763
Website: www.fortdavis.com/
attractions.html (link through Fort
Davis site)
Hours:
Tuesday–Saturday: Noon–4 p.m.
(often open until 5 p.m. on
Saturdays)
Closed Sunday

Selected Wines
Cabernet Sauvignon
Sauvignon Blanc
Blue Mountain Table White
Blue Mountain Table Red

At 5,400 feet above sea level, Blue Mountain is the highest winery in Texas. Up there, the air is cool and the scenery delightful. Mild temperatures allow for a longer growing season, which yields flavorful dark red grapes.

Patrick Johnson is the manager, winemaker, and grower on this twenty-acre vineyard owned by Nell Weisbach. Patrick, who has a degree in botany, enjoys the agricultural aspect of the wine business. He believes that taking care of the details out in the vineyard is a key ingredient in producing top-quality wines. Blue Mountain's grapes are carefully handpicked, and Patrick oversees every aspect of growing and wine production. He makes the final decision on when the wine is ready for bottling, which also takes place at the winery. Blue Mountain is known for its Cabernet Sauvignon, which has achieved high awards and recognition.

The vineyard site, Blue Mountain, consists of good rocky clay with permeability that allows the roots to dig far into the soil and enjoy the benefits of deep penetration. The plants thrive in the warm daytime temperatures and crisp, cool nights.

In its earliest days, the vineyard sold its grapes to other wineries, but that practice ended in 1994 with Blue Mountain's first vintage of Cabernet Sauvignon and Sauvignon Blanc. Today, Blue Mountain wines are sold at the winery and in select locations around Texas.

Blue Mountain's tasting room opened in September 2001, providing visitors to the area a chance to see this scenic vineyard. The Fort Davis area is a pleasant region to visit, with unique attractions including the McDonald Observatory and a number of hotels, quaint inns, and restaurants. The Hotel Limpia, in the heart of Fort Davis, is an ideal place for families. Amenities include generously sized rooms, spacious lounge areas, a fine restaurant, and gift shop featuring unique Texana items. During the summer, a pitcher of cold, freshly made lemonade is available for guests upon check-in.

Patrick provided this recipe, a favorite that he enjoys with his wife Deena.

Rosemary Leg of Lamb

Serves 8

Winemaker Patrick Johnson and his wife Deena enjoy this savory grilled lamb. Patrick and Deena grow their own rosemary, which thrives in the relatively dry weather of the West Texas high desert. This hearty dish marinates 24 hours and is best served with potatoes.

1 cup fresh rosemary
1 cup olive oil
Freshly ground pepper
1 leg of lamb roast

1. Mix rosemary, olive oil, and pepper; pour over lamb in large plastic bag. Make sure that the olive oil covers the lamb; add more as needed. Marinate 24 hours.
2. After marinating, grill lamb over relatively low heat for 45–50 minutes on gas grill, wood, or charcoal barbecue. Score the roast if it is thick so that it will cook all the way through.

Note: Lamb chops may be used in place of the leg of lamb roast.
Wine: Serve with Blue Mountain Cabernet Sauvignon.

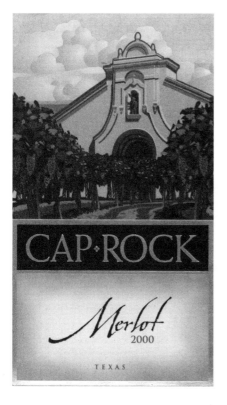

5

Cap*Rock Wineries

Lubbock and Grapevine, Texas

If you go . . .

Cap*Rock Winery in Lubbock

408 E. Woodrow Road
Lubbock, TX 79423
Phone: (806) 863-2704
Toll-free: (800) 546-9463
Website: www.caprockwinery.com
Hours: Monday–Saturday: 10 a.m.–5 p.m. (last tour at 4:30 p.m.)
Sunday: Noon–5 p.m.

Cap*Rock Winery at Grapevine

409 S. Main Street
Grapevine, TX 76051
Phone: (817) 329-9463
Website: www.caprockwinery.com
Hours:
Tuesday–Saturday: 11 a.m.–4:30 p.m.
Sunday: Noon 5 p.m.

Selected Wines

Tier I—Reserves:
Reserve Cabernet Sauvignon
Reserve Toscano Rosso
Reserve Orange Muscat
Reserve Merlot
Reserve Chardonnay
Cap*Rock Sparkling Blanc de Noir
Tier II—Varietals:
Cabernet Sauvignon
Chardonnay
Merlot
Tier III—Proprietary Wines:
Cabernet Royale, Rose of Cabernet
    Sauvignon
Topaz Royale
Vintners Red, Red Table Wine
Vintners White, White Table Wine
Vintners Blush, Texas Table Wine

The Cap*Rock Winery in Lubbock is a breathtaking southwestern mission-style structure set in the midst of open plains that stretch as far as the eye can see. The 23,000-square-foot main building, which opened in 1992, is an idyllic setting for a wedding.

Cap*Rock gets its name from the geology of the High Plains region. The winery sits at an elevation of 3,400 feet and has 120 acres of vineyards. Grape varieties grown in its vineyards include Cabernet Sauvignon, Merlot, Cabernet Franc, Malbec, Sangiovese, Barbera, Chardonnay, Sauvignon Blanc, Chenin Blanc, and Orange Muscat.

Tours take visitors through the entire winemaking process, beginning with the area where grapes are loaded from gondolas into the winery. Visitors see the tunnels that transport the grapes for destemming and crushing, and they walk through cool cellars laced with the delicious scent of fermenting wine. The bottling area offers a chance to see this important function of fermenting, which is monitored by winemaker Kim McPherson. Kim is a veteran of the wine industry. His father, known to many as "Doc" McPherson (for his experience as a chemistry professor), is a founder of the wine industry in Texas. Kim studied oenology at the University of California at Davis, and has extensive experience working with wines. Cap*Rock wines earn prestigious awards under his direction.

After bottling, the final stop before the tasting room is the grandiose barrel room, which boasts tall ceilings and cedar walls that trap the heat at the top of the room and lower the room's humidity.

Guests step out of the barrel room and into the tasting area to sample some of Cap*Rock's award-winning wines. The winery produces three tiers of wines. Tier I includes the reserve wines, such as Toscano Rosso, an award-winning Italian style wine. Tier II features varietals, such as Chardonnay and Sauvignon Blanc. Tier III includes the proprietary wines, such as the table wines.

A well-stocked gift shop is adjacent to the tasting bar. There, you can peruse the wide selection of wine-related accessories, T-shirts, and fine gift items.

Cap*Rock has ample space for special events in the tasting room or outdoors on the covered patio. The winery boasts a full-size kitchen so caterers can prepare items on-site.

The Cap*Rock Wine Club offers many benefits for members, including discounts and admission to special events in Lubbock and Grapevine, Texas, where Cap*Rock has a tasting room and retail operation. The Grapevine location offers visitors the opportunity to sample and purchase Cap*Rock's wines and accessories.

Steve Wilson from Cap*Rock Winery provides the following recipes. He extends credit for recipe development to Dustin Sockwell.

Sweet and Spicy Chicken

Serves 4

This dish is delightful served on a bed of long-grain rice with a side of summer squash or asparagus.

4 boneless, skinless chicken breasts
1/4 cup cayenne pepper
1/3 cup brown sugar
2 cups long-grain rice
Salt and pepper
1/2 cup Reserve Cap*Rock Orange Muscat

1. Mix together brown sugar and Orange Muscat until they form a paste. Set aside.
2. Apply a generous helping of cayenne pepper, salt, and black pepper to both sides of chicken breasts.
3. Begin grilling the chicken over low to medium flame.
4. When the chicken is almost done, apply the paste of brown sugar and Muscat to coat both sides of the chicken breasts. Remove the chicken as it begins to caramelize.

Wine: Serve with Cap*Rock Chardonnay.

 ## Pepper Cab Steak

Serves 4

Prepare a Caesar salad and twice-baked potatoes to accompany these flavorful steaks. Start marinating the meat the night before serving.

4 rib-eye or T-bone steaks (1 to 1 1/2 inches thick)
1 bottle Cap*Rock Cabernet Sauvignon
5 cups peppercorns (partially ground)
1 clove garlic
4 sprigs cilantro

1. Marinate steaks overnight in the Cabernet Sauvignon, making sure meat is fully covered.

2. When ready to grill, cut 3 slits on each side of each steak, about ¼ inch deep.

3. Cut garlic clove into small slices. Stuff garlic and cilantro into each cut on the steaks.

4. Roll steak edges in partially crushed peppercorns and immediately place on grill.

5. Cook to desired doneness; we suggest medium rare.

Wine: Serve with Cap*Rock Toscano Rosso.

 ## Fiesta Chicken

Serves 4

Serve up a festive plate by accompanying the chicken with Spanish rice and black beans.

4 boneless, skinless chicken breasts
One 4-ounce can chopped green chilies
1 red bell pepper
1 yellow bell pepper
1 medium onion
1 cup sliced mushrooms
1 pound Velveeta cheese
1 can Rotel tomatoes and green chilies
1 bottle Cap*Rock Topaz Royale
Tony Chachere's Seasoning

1. Slice bell peppers and onion. Mix with sliced mushrooms.

2. Marinate chicken and vegetables separately in Topaz Royale for 2 hours.

3. While marinating, mix Velveeta, Rotel, and green chilies in large microwaveable bowl or slow cooker. Heat until cheese is completely melted.

4. Preheat oven to 350°F.

5. Sprinkle Tony Chachere's Seasoning on both sides of chicken and bake in preheated oven.

6. In a large skillet, sauté vegetables until tender.

7. When chicken is done, top each breast with vegetables and cheese mixture.

Wine: Serve with Cap*Rock Topaz Royale.

 ## Garlic-Crusted Tilapia

Serves 4

Serve with wild rice and a fresh vegetable medley.

4 tilapia fillets
4 garlic cloves
2 cups bread crumbs
2 cups Cap*Rock Chardonnay
Fresh cilantro
$1/8$ cup fresh-squeezed lemon juice
1 stick (4 oz.) butter

1. Preheat oven to 350°F.

2. Chop garlic very fine.

3. In saucepan, melt a small amount of the butter. Sauté garlic until slightly browned. Add remaining butter, and the Chardonnay, lemon juice, and cilantro. Bring mixture to a boil. Let sauce simmer until the wine is reduced by half.

4. Mix bread crumbs into sauce, forming a moist but solid mixture.

5. Coat tilapia fillets with breading. Bake until done, usually about 20 minutes.

Wine: Serve with Cap*Rock Chardonnay.

 Blushing Fruits Dessert

Serves 10–12

1 angel food cake
1 cup sliced strawberries
1 cup raspberries
1 cup blueberries
1 cup mandarin oranges
2 cups Cap*Rock Blush Royale
¼ cup sugar
2 cups heavy cream, whipped

1. In large bowl, combine fruits with sugar and Blush Royale. Chill in refrigerator 3 to 4 hours.

2. Cut cake into individual servings and place on plates. Top with fruit mixture and whipped cream.

Wine: Serve with Cap*Rock Blush Royale.

6

Chisholm Trail Winery

Fredericksburg, Texas

If you go . . .

Chisholm Trail Winery

2367 Usener Road
Fredericksburg, TX 78624
Phone: (830) 990-CORK (2675)
Toll-free: (877) 990-2675
Website:
www.chisholmtrailwinery.com
Hours:
Thursday–Monday: Noon–6 p.m.
Closed Tuesday and Wednesday

Chisholm Trail Bed and Breakfast

1403 Main Street
Fredericksburg, TX 78624
Phone: (830) 990-2675

Selected Wines

Cabernet Sauvignon
Late Harvest Cabernet Sauvignon
(dessert wine)
Silver Spur (Cabernet/Merlot blend)
Merlot
Rosé (made from Cabernet Franc)
Chenin Blanc
Ghostrider (White Merlot)

Chisholm Trail Winery is tucked into a valley that lies to the west of Fredericksburg in the Texas Hill Country. The winery started making wine for the general public in 1999, and released its first vintage two years later. Grapes are grown on the twenty-three-acre Spring Creek Vineyard site adjacent to the winery. Paula K. Williamson and Harry Skeins Jr., both attorneys from San Antonio, bought the land in 1992, a purchase that was the fulfillment of a dream that arose during trips to Germany and Italy, where the two gained an appreciation for European wines.

When they first starting growing grapes, Harry and Paula hired a consultant, the late Vernon Gold, to help with their initial planting. They started small, planting just five acres of Cabernet Sauvignon grapes in 1994. Additional acreage was planted each year until 1998, when they reached their current level of twenty-three acres. Harry Skeins Jr. serves as vineyard manager, working the land to ensure that top-quality grapes are grown.

Chisholm Trail wines are sold at many locations throughout Texas. Guests are encouraged to visit the winery and enjoy a picnic at the nearby creek while savoring gourmet picnic fare sold at the Chisholm Trail General Store. Unique gift items and dining accessories are also available at the shop.

The winery participates in the Hill Country Wine Trail events, and offers other innovative programs for visitors. The owners celebrate the winery's birthday and other holidays such as Independence Day in grand style with entertainment, a gourmet menu, and of course their wines. The 2003 Independence Day celebration (held Saturday, July 5) featured complimentary hors d'oeuvres, wine freezies, watermelon, live music, and the poetry of "trail boss" Harry Skeins Jr. The Chisholm Trail website includes a complete list of events.

The Chisholm Trail Bed and Breakfast is located on Fredericksburg's Main Street. Two four-room suites offer couples a chance to unwind and relax in rooms that include a kitchenette, private bath featuring a claw-foot bathtub, and a private patio.

There are exciting expansion plans at Chisholm Trail, including an additional bed and breakfast, a wedding chapel, and a delicatessen.

Paula offers the following two beverage recipes—one provides a refreshing summertime chill, the other offers warmth in the winter months.

 ## Chisholm Trail Glühwein

Serves 8–10

On a cold day, snuggle up with a mug of this spicy concoction.

One 750-ml bottle Chisholm Trail Rosé
1½ cups cranberry-raspberry juice
3 cinnamon sticks
1 tablespoon whole cloves
1 medium orange, sliced with peel
1 small lemon, sliced with peel
½ cup sugar

1. Mix together all ingredients in a large saucepan. (It is recommended that you place the cinnamon sticks and cloves in a cheesecloth or spice bag while heating).
2. Cook over medium heat until steaming hot, but not boiling.

Chisholm Trail Wine Freezies

Serves 4

These wine slushes are a refreshing alternative to a frozen margarita.

One 6-ounce can limeade concentrate
One 6-ounce can filled with Chisholm Trail Rosé (Pour
    from bottle into the empty limeade can to measure.)
6 ounces club soda
One 6-ounce can strawberry daiquiri–margarita mix
3 cups ice

1. Mix all ingredients in blender. Blend until mixture has a slushy consistency.
2. Serve in a margarita glass with sugar around the rim.

Delaney Vineyards

Grapevine and Lamesa, Texas

If you go . . .

Delaney Vineyards at Grapevine

2000 Champagne Blvd.
Grapevine, TX 76051
Phone: (817) 481-5668
Website: www.delaneyvineyards.com
Retail shop hours:
Monday–Saturday: 10 a.m.–5 p.m.
Tours and wine tastings: Saturday:
Noon–5 p.m. (Sometimes closes
earlier on Saturday to accommodate
special events. Call to determine
hours.)

Delaney Vineyards at Lamesa

Highway 137 (1 mile north of
Lamesa)
Lamesa, TX 79331
Phone: (806) 872-3177
Hours: Tours and tastings by
appointment.

Selected Wines

Texas Claret (Cabernet Sauvignon,
   Cabernet Franc blend)
Sauvignon Blanc
Chardonnay
Texas White (Chardonnay)
Texas Rosé (Chardonnay, Cabernet
   Franc blend)
Barrel Fermented Chardonnay
Cabernet Sauvignon
Cabernet Franc
Merlot
Muscat Canelli
Texas Champagne Brut

Jerry Delaney grew up on West Texas land so it is no wonder that some of his favorite moments are spent cruising his vineyards in a tractor. In the town of Lamesa (Jerry made sure I understood that it is pronounced "lah-MEE-sah"), Delaney's family has farmed since they started growing cotton in the 1890s. Jerry worked the fields as a young boy, and his love of the soil and appreciation for farming spurred a desire in the entrepreneurial Delaney to grow premium grapes and produce top-quality wines. He has achieved his goal.

In 1983, Jerry planted his first harvest. Today, Delaney Vineyards has about 100 acres of grapes growing in Lamesa and another 10 acres in Grapevine. Lamesa, Texas, at an altitude of 3,200 feet, has a climate conducive to growing grapes. The fruit basks in the summertime heat and cools down at night when the sun dips over a ridge.

Although the Lamesa facility is available to tourists, the Grapevine operation is the winery's primary tourist destination. The magnificent facility, located just a stone's throw from Dallas-Fort Worth Airport, is reminiscent of eighteenth-century French architecture. Inside, the grandiose 5,200-square-foot barrel room boasts a forty-foot vaulted ceiling and Italian granite tasting bar. The room accommodates 250 people for a sit-down function, or 400 for a cocktail affair.

Outside, a 1,500-square-foot patio overlooking the vineyard welcomes guests, rain or shine. Fans, heaters, and roll-down sunshades keep partygoers comfortable during the special events scheduled at the winery. Delaney Vineyards hosts its own events, as well as private weddings and other ceremonies and galas. The winery building also houses a gift shop with a unique collection of wine accessories, and of course the wines themselves.

A major special event held each August in Grapevine is Delaney's "Grape Stomp." Entire families are encouraged to come out and participate in the festivities. The event begins in the morning when guests pick grapes right off the vine using a special tool. Rows and rows of vines bursting with grapes stand ready to be picked by eager families.

Then it's time to stomp. Guests are invited to take off their shoes and romp around in a large grape-filled basin. The squishy grapes underfoot provide a sensation all their own. Dance and waddle through knee-high grapes with entertainment by Lucy and Ethel look-alikes. It's "grape fun" for all! The event also features wine sampling (kiddy "wine" for the young folks), an art fair, and hayrides.

Winemaking at Delaney is done under the direction of Bénédicte Rhyne, a native of France who worked as a winemaker in California's Sonoma Valley before moving to Texas in 2001. Bénédicte has had extensive training in the study of wine and chemistry and is a perfectionist, a trait that carries through to the Delaney wines, which have received numerous awards and accolades. A gourmet chef, Bénédicte has developed the following recipes to complement Delaney wines and champagne. For a twist on the traditional champagne cocktail, Bénédicte suggests placing a few plump red raspberries at the bottom of each flute before filling to the brim with Delaney Champagne Brute, a delightful champagne made by the méthode champenoise.

 Grilled Shrimp and Sea Scallop Skewers

Serves 6

These popular appetizers were developed by Delaney's winemaker, Bénédicte Rhyne.

Thirty 10-inch wood skewers
15 large shrimp
15 large sea scallops, cleaned and rinsed
Olive oil
Salt and pepper to taste

1. Cover wood skewers with cold water 3 hours prior to cooking to prevent them from burning.
2. Prepare grill and spray with a nonstick cooking spray (or preheat broiler if grill is not available).
3. Place one scallop or one shrimp on each skewer. Make sure skewer goes through head and tail of shrimp. Lightly brush with olive oil and season with salt and pepper.
4. Grill seafood on each side for 2 to 3 minutes (or broil 1 to 2 minutes) until done.
5. Serve hot or at room temperature with homemade cocktail sauce.

Homemade Cocktail Sauce:

1 cup ketchup
1/2 cup horseradish sauce
2 tablespoons lemon juice
1/2 teaspoon Tabasco sauce
Dash of Worcestershire sauce
Parsley, roughly chopped
Lemon slices

1. Reserve lemon slices and parsley. Mix remaining ingredients in a bowl.
2. Garnish sauce with parsley. Serve with lemon slices.

Wine: Serve with Delaney Texas Champagne Brut.

Crab-Filled Tomatoes

Serves 6–8

Bénédicte Rhyne from Delaney Vineyards offers these delicious appetizers to complement any cocktail hour.

½ pound crabmeat
1 tablespoon mayonnaise
2 tablespoons crème fraîche (or sour cream)
1 tablespoon fresh tarragon, chopped
Salt and pepper, to taste
30 small cherry tomatoes
1 bunch chives, chopped (Reserve several unchopped, for garnish.)

1. Rinse crabmeat and drain. Wrap in a clean tea towel and wring to remove any remaining moisture. Transfer to a bowl.
2. Mix mayonnaise and crème fraîche, adding crabmeat and tarragon. Add salt and pepper to taste.
3. Remove top third of each tomato, then top with a pinch of crabmeat mixture. Chill up to 2 hours. Let sit at room temperature for 30 minutes before serving.
4. Garnish with chives and transfer to platter. You can arrange the platter with stalks of savory chives in a cheery checkerboard pattern.

Wine: Serve with Delaney Texas Champagne Brut.

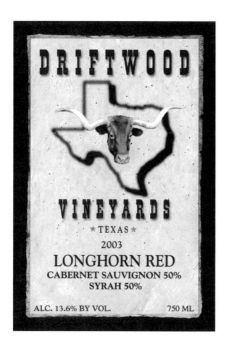

Driftwood Vineyards

Driftwood, Texas

If you go . . .
Driftwood Vineyards
21550 Ranch Road 12
Driftwood, TX 78619
Phone: (512) 692-6229
Website:
www.driftwoodvineyards.com
Hours:
Monday–Saturday: 10 a.m.–6 p.m.
Sunday: noon–6 p.m.

Selected Wines
Chardonnay
Viognier
Armadillo Red (Sangiovese)
Longhorn Red (Cabernet/Sangiovese blend)
Lone Star Cab (estate-grown Cabernet Sauvignon)

Driftwood Vineyards overlooks the surrounding Hill Country from its perch on a hill just west of Austin. There, Gary, Kathy, and Laura Elliott operate the eighteen-acre vineyard, which grows eight grape varieties.

Kathy's father purchased this breathtaking property in 1951; the Elliotts planted their first grapes in 1998. Initially, the vineyard's county was dry, so the family sold their grapes to other wineries. In 2001, new state legislation allowed wineries to sell their wines at the winery itself, opening up new possibilities for Driftwood Vineyards. The vineyard's first commercial grape crush was held in August 2002, and the Elliotts bottled their first commercial wines six months later. On March 1, 2003, they opened the winery to visitors. That first year was a busy one, resulting in the production of 1,200 bottles featuring five different wine varieties. Driftwood began winning awards for its wines within its first year of operation.

In summer 2003, a sprawling deck opened just outside the tasting room, providing guests the opportunity to take in the spectacular Hill Country and vineyard view and enjoy the fresh country air. The winery began offering Saturday and Sunday lunches in 2003. Prepared by a local delicatessen, the selections feature items that complement Driftwood Vineyards wines. Lunch for a group may be arranged by calling ahead.

The vineyard offers a number of special events throughout the year, including wine classes, weddings, and other gatherings.

The Elliotts' property stretches through 900 acres with the South Gatlin Creek winding through it. A private house located near the vineyard features a bed and breakfast with two bedrooms and two baths, living and dining rooms, kitchen, and family room complete with a pool table and fireplace for those chilly Hill Country nights. The website offers more details and photos of the vineyard and overnight accommodations.

Laura's Chicken Piccata

Serves 2

Serve these flavorful chicken cutlets with basmati rice and a fresh steamed vegetable.

Season: 4 chicken cutlets
Sauté in: 2 tablespoons vegetable oil
Deglaze with:

> ¼ cup dry white wine or low-sodium chicken broth
> 1 teaspoon garlic, minced

Add:

> ½ cup low-sodium chicken broth (or more, for additional sauce)
> 2 tablespoons fresh lemon juice
> 3 tablespoons capers, drained
> Sautéed cutlets

Finish with:

> 2 tablespoons unsalted butter
> Fresh lemon slices

Garnish with: Chopped fresh parsley

1. Prepare two boneless, skinless chicken breasts for cutlets by gently pounding each half breast between two pieces

of plastic wrap to a uniform thickness of ¹/₄ inch. Season cutlets with salt and pepper, then dust with flour.

2. Spray a sauté pan with nonstick cooking spray. Add vegetable oil and heat over medium-high heat.

3. Sauté cutlets for 2 to 3 minutes on one side. Turn cutlets over and sauté the other side for 1 to 2 minutes with the pan covered, until they are golden brown on each side. Transfer to a warm plate; pour off fat from the pan.

4. Deglaze pan with wine or chicken broth, and add minced garlic. Cook until the garlic is *slightly* brown and the liquid is nearly gone, about 2 minutes.

5. Add broth, lemon juice, and capers. Return cutlets to pan and cook on each side for 1 minute. Transfer cutlets to warm plate.

6. Finish with butter and lemon slices. Once butter melts, pour sauce over cutlets.

7. Garnish with fresh chopped parsley.

Wine: Serve with Driftwood Vineyards Chardonnay or Viognier.

Dry Comal Creek Vineyards

New Braunfels, Texas

If you go . . .

Dry Comal Creek Vineyards
1741 Herbelin Road
New Braunfels, TX 78132
Phone: (830) 885-4121
Website: www.drycomalcreek.com
Hours:
Wednesday–Sunday: Noon–5 p.m.
Closed Monday and Tuesday

Selected Wines
Cabernet Sauvignon
Merlot
Chardonnay
Sauvignon Blanc
French Colombard (bone-dry)
French Colombard (demi-sweet)
Comal Red III

Dry Comal Creek Vineyards is tucked into a protected Hill Country valley. There, proprietors Franklin D. and Bonnie Houser offer personal care and attention to grape growing and production of their award-winning wines.

The Housers take a "handmade approach to picking, fermentation, winemaking and bottling," and invite visitors to tour the scenic winery and sample the wines. The winery participates in a number of special events throughout the year. The

Housers are included in Hill Country wine trail events, and they host many gatherings at the vineyard. Bonnie Houser is a gourmet cook who enjoys collecting recipes. She shares four of her favorite recipes from the vineyard.

Spinach-Basil Cheese Ball

Makes one 5-inch cheese ball

*This recipe is shared with permission from my friend's cookbook—*Tea Treasures and More, *by Carol Sims. Sometimes I double the cheeses, if I want an extra large ball.—Bonnie Houser*

> 8 ounces cream cheese
> 4 ounces goat cheese (provincial)
> 1 cup fresh baby spinach leaves
> 1 cup fresh basil
> 1/4 cup olive oil
> 2 cloves garlic
> 1/2 cup grated Parmesan cheese
> Pepper to taste
> 1/2 cup pine nuts or almonds (roasted)
> 1/2 cup dried cranberries or sundried tomatoes packed in oil

1. Place spinach leaves, basil, olive oil, and garlic in food processor. Mix until smooth. Add Parmesan cheese and pepper.
2. Blend the cream cheese and goat cheese together in an electric mixer until smooth.
3. Line a small 5-inch bowl with plastic wrap. Spray inside the wrap with nonstick cooking spray. Line with half of the cream cheese mixture. Add the entire basil mixture, and the

pine nuts and cranberries. Top with the remaining cream cheese mixture. Cover lined bowl with plastic wrap. Refrigerate for at least 30 minutes (several hours is preferred).

4. Unwrap and serve upside down on a plate with lavash crackers.

Bonnie's Suggestions for Modifying the Recipe: Add 1 tablespoon "Franklin's Fire Roasted Herbs," sold at Dry Comal Creek Vineyards, to the cheeses for more flavor and piquancy. Double cheeses for an extra large ball. Garnish top with parsley, roasted bell pepper cut into shapes, or edible flowers.

Wine: Serve with Dry Comal Creek Vineyards bone-dry French Colombard or Sauvignon Blanc.

Paul Ideker's Baked Grapes and Red Onion Conserve

Serves 12 (as an appetizer)

This recipe was shared with me by Paul Ideker, whom I met in Maine at an antique dealers' party. He brought the dish, and I asked for the recipe because of the grape/wine connection.—Bonnie Houser

3 cups red seedless grapes
1 medium red onion, chopped
Fresh thyme (the amount is up to you)
$^1/_4$–$^1/_2$ cup premium olive oil
1 cup chopped black olives
3 tablespoons balsamic vinegar

1. Preheat oven to 400°F.
2. Toss first three ingredients with olive oil.

3. Place in baking dish and bake in preheated oven for 45 minutes.

4. Remove from oven. Carefully drain off oil and cool to room temperature.

5. Mash grapes with a fork, and add olives and balsamic vinegar.

Serving Suggestion: Serve over mascarpone, goat, or cream cheese, with crackers or soda bread.

Wine: Serve with Dry Comal Creek Vineyards demi-sweet French Colombard.

 ### Ellie's Sunday Sausage

Serves 8-10

Men love this casserole! Serving it has become a family tradition on Christmas mornings at the vineyard. We serve it with cranberry scones and strawberry butter.—Bonnie Houser

2 cups celery, finely chopped
1 large onion, finely chopped
1 green pepper, finely chopped
1 red bell pepper, finely chopped
2 pounds Owens pork sausage (1 pound hot, 1 pound medium)
2 packages ($2^1/2$ ounces each) dehydrated chicken noodle soup
$^1/2$ cup uncooked rice
1 small jar (2 ounces) pimientos
2 cans (6 ounces each) sliced water chestnuts
3 cups boiling water

1. Preheat oven to 350°F.
2. Put dehydrated soup in large casserole. Carefully pour boiling water over soup and let stand.
3. Cook sausage, using two skillets, if needed, to brown well. Drain, reserving 2 tablespoons fat in pan. Sauté celery, onion, and peppers until light yellow in color.
4. Combine all ingredients, mixing well.
5. Cover and bake in preheated oven for 1 1/2 hours, stirring once after 30 minutes. If more liquid is needed, add a small amount of chicken stock or consommé.

Note: This casserole can be frozen before baking. Either bring it to room temperature before baking or add 30 minutes to the baking time. (If you are wondering about Ellie, Bonnie says that she is "a dear friend from the army days in Germany. She's the model hostess, exemplary cook, and always one to share her heart, home, and recipes.")

Wine: Serve with Mimosas made with fresh orange juice and Dry Comal Creek demi-sweet French Colombard (use equal parts of orange juice and French Colombard).

 ## Braised Beef with Cabernet and Brandy

Serves 6-8

This family favorite was adapted from the Samuel Chamberlain Calendar of French Cooking, 1962.—Bonnie Houser

$^1/_4$ stick butter

$2^1/_2$-pound rump or round of beef, cut in large pieces

$^3/_4$ to 1 cup brandy

8 to 10 small whole onions

4 slices bacon

$^1/_2$ cup warm water

1 to 2 teaspoons bouquet garni

2 cloves garlic

1 to 2 cups Dry Comal Creek Vineyards Cabernet
    Sauvignon

8 to 12 mushrooms

12 green, pitted Italian olives, blanched in boiling water

Salt and pepper to taste

1. Cook bacon until slightly done. Drain, pat dry, and chop into large pieces. Set aside.

2. Melt butter in a heavy casserole dish. Slowly brown beef well on all sides. Add brandy. Cover and simmer over low heat for 30 minutes.

3. Preheat oven to 300°F.

4. Add the onions, bacon, warm water, garlic, bouquet garni, salt, and pepper to the beef. Add 1 cup of the Cabernet.

5. Place in preheated oven for $2^1/_2$ hours, adding more brandy and Cabernet if needed, being careful not to let it get too dry.

6. After 2 hours, add mushrooms and olives.

Serving Suggestion: Noodles, rice, or potatoes make an ideal accompaniment to this hearty dish.

Wine: Serve with Dry Comal Creek Vineyards Merlot, Cabernet Sauvignon, or Black Spanish.

Fall Creek Vineyards

Tow, Texas

If you go . . .
Fall Creek Vineyards
1820 Co. Rd. 222
Tow, TX 78672
Phone: (325) 379-5361
Website: www.fcv.com
Hours:
Monday–Friday: 11 a.m.–4 p.m.
Saturday: Noon–5 p.m.
Sunday: Noon–4 p.m.
Call winery for holiday schedules.

Selected Wines
Chardonnay
Sauvignon Blanc
Cascade (Semillon, Sauvignon Blanc
   blend)
Chenin Blanc
Johannisberg Riesling
Meritus (Merlot, Cabernet
   Sauvignon, Malbec blend)
Muscat Canelli
Cabernet Sauvignon
Granite Reserve (Cabernet, Merlot,
   Malbec blend)
Granite Blush (Johannisberg Riesling,
   Chenin Blanc, Cabernet
   Sauvignon blend)
Merlot
Sweet Jo (dessert wine)

Texas businessman and rancher Ed Auler and his wife, Susan, formed Fall Creek Vineyards back in 1975 on a beautiful site in the Texas Hill Country, eighty miles north of Austin. One thousand people, including members of the press, musicians, and the general public flocked to Tow to help the Aulers celebrate the opening. Twenty years later, large crowds gathered again at the vineyard in Tow, this time to celebrate two decades of excellence in winemaking. A lot of excitement occurred during those years.

During its opening year, Fall Creek's first vintage Chenin Blanc ranked at the top of the "Wine and Spirits Buying Guide" for all Chenin Blancs across the nation. Two years later, Fall Creek Vineyards wines were among the fifty American wines served at an inaugural "Taste of America" dinner honoring President Reagan. In 1989 the wines were featured at another presidential inaugural dinner, this time in honor of President George Herbert Walker Bush. Later that same year,

Fall Creek Vineyards 1987 Cabernet Sauvignon and 1988 Sauvignon Blanc were airlifted to China, where they were served at a Texas-style barbecue hosted by President and First Lady Bush.

Perhaps you have heard of the Texas Hill Country Wine and Food Festival held each April? The Aulers founded and hosted the event in 1986. (Today the event is known as the Saveur Texas Hill Country Wine and Food Festival.)

The concept for Fall Creek Vineyards developed in the Aulers' minds while they were traveling in France. The topography and climate of the French countryside reminded them of the Texas Hill Country outside of Austin, and they wondered if they could create a vineyard on their ranch. The idea was born, the grapes were planted in 1975, and four years later the Aulers bottled their first wines.

The vineyard enjoys hot summertime days and cool nights, and the humidity usually stays low. Proximity to Lake Buchanan provides gentle breezes that cool the air.

Today, Fall Creek Vineyards produces a wide selection of white, red, and blush wines. The winery has undergone multiple expansions since those early days, and now includes a large visitors/tasting center. The setting at Tow provided inspiration for the late author James Michener, who stayed at Fall Creek Vineyards while writing the book, *Texas.*

The design for the massive 20,000-square-foot winery was developed by Susan Auler, who has a design degree from the University of Texas. Antique stable doors from the Louis Pasteur Laboratory near Paris, France, provide closure for a room housing the oak casks. While ancient artifacts create ambience, the most modern equipment is utilized in winemaking at Fall Creek Vineyards.

The winery's gift shop features the Fall Creek line of gourmet food products as well as a full selection of its outstanding wines. Food products include Cabernet Sauvignon Jelly, Cellar Select Mustard, and Fall Creek Salsa featuring the winery's Sauvignon Blanc. A more complete selection of the food items is provided on the website, with information on purchasing these and other gift items via mail order.

Fall Creek Vineyards hosts a number of special events throughout the year. The grape stomp is an annual event that began in 1988. In addition to the fun associated with stomping the grapes, guests enjoy Vanishing Texas River Cruises launched from the property's shore, vineyard hayrides, miniature train rides for the younger folks, wine tastings, winery tours, and many more activities. Fall Creek Vineyards participates in wine trail events as well.

Susan Auler, who celebrates the marriage of fine food and fine wine, graciously shares some of her favorite vineyard recipes.

Susan's Texas Pizza

Makes 10 appetizer servings

Susan Auler, co-owner of Fall Creek Vineyards, developed this recipe, which combines several ingredients dear to Texans' hearts: tortillas, chile pepper, and goat cheese. Using the tortilla as the pizza crust makes this a quick and easy appetizer. Grilled meats may be added for a heartier meal item.

    One 9- to 10-inch flour tortilla
    1 tablespoon poblano chile, minced
    1 tablespoon garlic, minced
    2 cups eggplant cubes ($^3/_8$-inch cubes without skin)

2 tablespoons unsalted butter
4 Roma tomatoes, seeded, skins removed
Salt, to taste
1 teaspoon fresh oregano, minced
4 teaspoons fresh cilantro, minced
6 ounces Texas goat cheese
1 avocado, sliced or chopped

1. Preheat oven to 350°F.
2. Score tortilla into 10 equal wedges with pizza cutter. Do not cut tortilla all the way through; this enables tortilla to be broken easily into wedges prior to serving.
3. Place tortilla in pie pan so that edges barely curl up sides of pan. Bake until light brown, approximately 10 minutes.
4. Mince chile and garlic; cube eggplant. Sauté chile, garlic, and eggplant in butter.
5. Puree tomatoes, salt, oregano, and cilantro in food processor.
6. Add tomato mixture to eggplant mixture. Continue to cook until mixture thickens and moisture evaporates.
7. Crumble goat cheese evenly on tortilla. Spoon hot tomato mixture on top of cheese.
8. Garnish with avocado slices or chopped avocado.

Wine: Serve with Fall Creek Vineyards Chenin Blanc or Granite Reserve.

Fall Creek Grilled Salmon with Avocado Béarnaise

Serves 4

Susan Auler, co-owner of Fall Creek Vineyards, developed this recipe, as she is a lover of salmon as well as picnics. This is a great picnic item when toting a grill.

1¼ pounds salmon fillet
1 tablespoon olive oil
Juice of one lemon
½ teaspoon salt
½ teaspoon freshly ground pepper

1. Remove any bones from salmon fillet. Drizzle top and skin side of salmon with olive oil. Drizzle lemon juice over top of salmon; salt and pepper evenly.
2. Place on hot grill, skin side down, and grill until just done (pink turns pale), approximately 10 minutes.
3. Serve immediately with béarnaise sauce.

Avocado Béarnaise Sauce:

3 tablespoons white wine
2 teaspoons garlic, minced
1½ tablespoons green onion, minced
3 tablespoons tarragon vinegar
¼ teaspoon pepper
4 egg yolks
1 teaspoon salt
3 teaspoons fresh cilantro, finely minced
¾ cup unsalted butter, melted
2 tablespoons fresh lemon juice
1 avocado, peeled and cubed

1. In a small skillet, combine wine, garlic, green onion, vinegar, and pepper. Boil rapidly until only about 2 table-spoons liquid remain. Set aside for addition to sauce.
2. In blender, blend egg yolks at high speed until thick. Add salt, cilantro, and ingredients from skillet. Add 4 table-

spoons hot melted butter, a little at a time, blending on high constantly. Beat in remaining butter alternately with lemon juice; add avocado and blend well.

3. Keep warm over hot water (or pack in a thermos for a picnic).

Wine: Serve with Fall Creek Chardonnay or Fall Creek Sauvignon Blanc.

Rice, Pecan, and Apricot Stuffing for Wild Turkey

Serves 6

Susan Auler, co-owner of Fall Creek Vineyards, developed this recipe to accompany the wild game that is hunted on the family's ranches.

1 cup rice
1 cup water
1 cup chicken broth
1 tablespoon butter
$1/2$ teaspoon salt
$1/4$ teaspoon coarse black pepper
$1/2$ cup butter
1 cup onion, chopped
$1/2$ cup mushrooms, sliced
1 cup dried apricots, minced
$1/2$ cup pecans, toasted

1. Cook rice with water, broth, butter, salt, and pepper until all liquid is dissolved.
2. Melt $1/2$ cup butter in skillet and sauté onions until golden. Add mushrooms and apricots. Cook until tender.

3. Add pecans and contents of skillet to rice.

4. Serve with wild turkey or other game fowl.

Wine: Serve with Fall Creek Vineyards Sauvignon Blanc or Fall Creek Vineyards Merlot.

 ## Chocolate Pear Tart

Serves 8–10

Susan Auler, co-owner of Fall Creek Vineyards, developed this unique dessert recipe. Susan loves chocolate and incorporates it into many of her recipes. Sometimes the chocolate predominates, and at other times it is in the background, as in this tart. Pears are a favorite fruit of the Auler family and are grown on the family estate.

For Tart Crust:

1¼ cups Wondra flour
¼ teaspoon salt
6 tablespoons cold unsalted butter, cut into small pieces
2 tablespoons corn oil
3 tablespoons ice water

1. In large bowl, mix flour and salt. Cut in cold butter. Blend in corn oil and ice water, and toss mixture to form ball. Knead dough lightly to distribute fat evenly and re-form into ball. Dust dough with flour and roll to fit tart pan. Chill dough in tart pan for 1 hour or more.

2. Preheat oven to 400°F.

3. Line tart shell with foil and weight down with rice or beans.

4. Bake for 15 minutes in preheated oven. Remove from oven. Remove foil and rice, and return to oven for 5 more minutes to brown bottom. Remove from oven and cool.

For Tart Topping:

1 cup bread crumbs
$1/2$ cup pine nuts
$1/4$ cup unsalted butter, cut into small pieces
$1/2$ cup brown sugar

1. Combine all ingredients in food processor, and process until consistency of oatmeal.
2. Set aside for later use.

For Raspberry Purée:

$1 1/2$ cups fresh raspberries
3 tablespoons maple syrup
2 tablespoons sugar

1. Simmer all ingredients until thickened, and pour through fine strainer.
2. Set aside.

For Tart Filling:

4 ounces semisweet chocolate
1 ounce unsalted butter
4 pears, peeled and sliced
1 lemon

1. Melt chocolate and butter in small skillet.
2. Line bottom of baked tart shell with chocolate mixture.
3. Arrange pear slices in concentric circles on top of chocolate in tart shell.
4. Squeeze juice from lemon evenly over top of pears.
5. Sprinkle topping mixture over pears.
6. Reduce oven temperature to 350°F. Bake 30 minutes. Serve warm with raspberry purée.

Wine: Serve with Fall Creek Vineyards Sweet Johannisberg Riesling ("Sweet Jo," which was named for the winery cat) or Twin Springs Sweet Wine.

Pecan Fudge Pie with Raspberry Purée

Serves 8

Susan Auler, co-owner of Fall Creek Vineyards, developed this recipe for family and friends to take with them on their many picnic outings.

For Fudge Pie:

¹/₂ cup butter
2 ounces unsweetened chocolate squares
1 cup sugar
¹/₂ cup flour
¹/₄ teaspoon salt
²/₃ cup toasted, chopped pecans
2 large eggs
1 teaspoon vanilla

1. Preheat oven to 350°F.
2. In small pan, melt butter and chocolate over low heat. Turn off heat and add sugar. Butter a pie plate.
3. Combine flour, salt, and pecans. Blend into butter, chocolate, sugar mixture.
4. Whisk eggs into chocolate and flour mixture. Add vanilla. Pour mixture into buttered pie plate.
5. Bake in preheated oven approximately 25 minutes. Check doneness by inserting a toothpick, which will come out clean when pie is done.

For Raspberry Purée:

2 cups fresh raspberries
3 tablespoons maple syrup
2 tablespoons sugar

1. Simmer 1½ cups raspberries, syrup, and sugar until thickened.
2. Pour through fine strainer.
3. To serve, pool on plate and place a slice of fudge pie on top. Garnish with remaining raspberries.

Wine: Serve with Fall Creek Vineyards Sweet Jo or Twin Springs Sweet Red.

Flat Creek Estate Vineyard & Winery

Marble Falls, Texas

If you go . . .
Flat Creek Estate Vineyard & Winery
24912 #1 Singleton Bend East
Marble Falls, TX 78654
Phone: (512) 267-6310
Website: www.flatcreekestate.com
Hours:
Tuesday–Friday: Noon–5 p.m.
Saturday: 10 a.m.–5 p.m.
Sunday: Noon–5 p.m.
Group tours available by appointment.

Selected Wines
Travis Peak Select Cabernet
  Sauvignon
Travis Peak Select Due Ami
  (Semillon/Sauvignon Blanc)
Travis Peak Select Muscato D'Arancia
Flat Creek Estate Muscato Blanco
Flat Creek Estate Sangiovese

The Texas Hill Country provides a spectacular backdrop to this charming winery reminiscent of Tuscany.

Owners Rick and Madelyn Naber found the property while riding through the scenic Hill Country. Prior to opening Flat Creek, Rick had a long and rewarding career in commercial construction, and Madelyn worked in health and exercise physiology. They now grow twelve acres of Italian/Mediterranean varietal grapes. In 2003, Flat Creek Estate released its first estate-grown wines, including Sangiovese, Primitivo (considered the "mother of Zinfandel"), and Port. Flat Creek wines have already received awards.

The first section of the vineyard, a six-acre piece of land called Helen's Home Block, was planted in 2000 and harvested for production in 2001. The three varieties planted in Helen's Home Block include Sangiovese, Primitivo, and Santa Madeira. A large group of volunteers helped plant and harvest. In 2002, even larger numbers of volunteers turned out for the harvest of the vineyard's first Muscat Blanc.

In another section, Hilltop Block, Shiraz grapes were planted in 2001 and harvested for the first time in 2003. Again, friends and neighbors helped Rick and Madelyn plant and harvest. Also in 2001, Pecan Park Block was first planted, featuring Pinot Grigio and additional Muscat Blanc grapes. This block was first harvested for production in 2003.

Nursery Block, used for developing vines for future grafting, is adjacent to Hilltop Block.

Flat Creek Estate offers two product lines, Flat Creek Estate Reserve label wines and Travis Peak Select wines. Flat Creek Estate Reserve wines represent the estate-grown wines, while Travis Peak Select wines feature some grapes from other high-quality Texas growers.

Each year after the harvest, the Nabers refer to the winery as the "center of the universe" at Flat Creek Estate. There, winemaker Craig D. Parker oversees the production. Craig grew up in the Australian wine industry and completed his studies in his home country. A winemaker and viticulturalist, Craig has also applied his skills in other countries including France, Germany, Italy, and New Zealand before coming to the United States, where he spent time working in the California wine industry. He first met Rick and Madelyn at a wine symposium, and was interested in working at Flat Creek, with its high-energy environment and strong commitment to quality. Clay Snodgrass, who has a background developing and maintaining premier golf courses, serves as vineyard manager.

Weddings, Tuscan dinners, wine trail events, cooking classes, and many other programs are held throughout the year at Flat Creek. The Vintner's Quarters, a bed and breakfast, offers overnight accommodations. Guests are encouraged to bring a picnic and enjoy the breathtaking scenery while hiking the vineyard trail. Ultimately, Flat Creek will grow to become a destination resort featuring a full line of guest amenities. Each year, usually coinciding with Valentine's Day, Flat Creek presents a wine release dinner, highlighting the year's newest vintages. Flat Creek's website offers a complete list of events, including wine trail programs.

Rick, Madelyn, and winemaker Craig Parker share three delightful recipes from the vineyard. A fourth recipe was served at one of Flat Creek Estate's special events, a dinner presented by visiting Italian chef Sylvia Sgarbossa. Buono appetito!

Apricot-Oatmeal Cookies

Makes about 4 dozen cookies

Madelyn Naber often serves these tasty home-baked cookies in Flat Creek Estate's tasting room.

1 cup butter
1¼ cups brown sugar
½ cup granulated sugar
2 eggs
2 tablespoons milk
2 teaspoons vanilla
1¾ cup + 2 tablespoons flour
1 teaspoon baking soda
½ teaspoon salt
2½ cups quick-cooking oats
1 cup dried apricots, diced
1 cup chopped walnuts

1. Preheat oven to 375°F.
2. Beat together butter and sugars until creamy. Add eggs, milk, and vanilla. Beat well.
3. Combine flour, baking soda, and salt. Add to butter

mixture. Mix well. Stir in oats, apricots, and nuts until thoroughly mixed.

4. Drop by spoonfuls onto ungreased cookie sheet, about 2 inches apart.

5. Bake 9–10 minutes in preheated oven. Cool briefly on sheet before removing with spatula.

 ## Uncle Charlie's Shepherd's Pie

Makes 1 pie

You will enjoy the play between the shepherd's pie's creamy, rich texture and the Flat Creek Estate Travis Peak Select Cabernet's rich, dark berry fruits and fine grain tannins. This is an old Australian home-style favorite shared by Flat Creek's winemaker, Craig D. Parker. Its robust flavors and hearty contents are ideal after a long day working in the vineyard. The recipe can be multiplied for additional pies. For best results, prepare one day before serving.

For Shepherd's Pie Casing:

> 1 1/2 to 2 1/2 cups dry mashed potato (potato that has been cooked and mashed, no butter, milk, or seasoning added)
> 1 teaspoon olive oil
> 1 egg, lightly beaten
> Kosher salt and fresh-cracked black pepper, to season
> 1 egg, lightly beaten with 1 teaspoon water to make egg wash

1. Beat mashed potato with wooden spoon until smooth.
2. Add oil, egg, and seasoning. Beat all ingredients together until smooth with no lumps. Set aside.

For Egg Wash: Beat 1 egg lightly with 1 teaspoon water, and set aside.

For Shepherd's Pie Filling:

3 lamb shanks
2 teaspoons oil
2 teaspoons butter
1/2 celery stalk, chopped
1/2 carrot, chopped
2 cloves garlic, minced
1 bay leaf
1 sprig fresh rosemary, finely chopped
1 sprig fresh lemon thyme, stripped from stalk and finely chopped
2 to 3 cups lamb stock (or one half beef and one half vegetable stock)
1 cup Travis Peak Select Due Ami

1. Heat butter and oil in heavy saucepan or casserole dish. Add lamb shanks and brown on all sides. Add vegetables, garlic, herbs, stock, and Due Ami until shanks are just covered. Bring to a boil. Cover and simmer 1 to 1 1/2 hours, until meat is tender and falls off bone.
2. Remove meat, strain, and cool the stock. Adjust seasonings to taste.
3. Cut meat into chunks, 1 inch or so in size. Return to stock. Refrigerate 1 hour or until needed.

To Assemble the Pie:

1. Place 2 3/4- to 3-inch diameter metal ring on greased baking sheet. Press some of the shepherd's pie casing across

the bottom and up and around the inside of the ring. Leave metal ring on at this stage. Fill center with some drained shepherd's pie filling. Finish pies by covering top of filling with more shepherd's pie casing. Brush top with egg wash and refrigerate for 1 hour.

2. Preheat oven to 400°F.

3. Place pie in preheated oven. Bake about 15 minutes or until skewer in center comes out hot.

Serving Suggestion: Serve with lamb gravy (use reserved drained stock and a thickening agent, such as flour or cornstarch) and steamed fresh peas with mint leaves and butter.
Wine: Serve with Flat Creek Estate Travis Peak Select current release Cabernet Sauvignon.

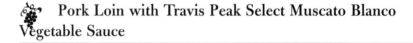

Pork Loin with Travis Peak Select Muscato Blanco Vegetable Sauce

Serves 6

Flat Creek Estate's own Rick Naber loves to prepare foods on the grill. He also enjoys experimental dishes, and created this sauce for a "Fourth Friday at Flat Creek Estate," a celebratory evening for the entire Flat Creek family.

Six 1-inch thick pork loins, butterflied
1¹/₂ cups carrots, grated
³/₄ cup sweet onion, diced
¹/₄ cup each of butter and olive oil
2 cups Flat Creek Estate Travis Peak Select Muscato Blanco
¹/₂ teaspoon coriander
¹/₂ teaspoon seasoned salt

¹/₂ teaspoon allspice

2 tablespoons brown sugar

2 tablespoons maple syrup

1. Grill pork loins (seasoned to taste) on the grill, turning frequently.

2. Sauté carrots and onions in butter and olive oil until onions are clear and carrots are soft in texture.

3. Add remaining ingredients and simmer on low heat until the sauce is the consistency desired for serving. (If tempted, add a pinch of this or a dash of that, and know that Chef Rick does the same.)

4. Serve over grilled chops.

Serving Suggestion: Excellent served with buttered red potatoes and steamed asparagus.

Wine: Serve with Travis Peak Select Muscato Blanco.

Pere al Travis Peak Select Cabernet Sauvignon

Serves 6

Chef Sylvia Sgarbossa visited Flat Creek Estate from her restaurant in Veneto, Italy. While at the winery, she prepared two special weekend meals and presented a cooking class. This poached pear dessert, now a classic favorite for Flat Creek family and guests, was served at one of the weekend dinners.

6 medium pears, peeled, halved, and cored
5 tablespoons sugar
One 750 ml bottle Travis Peak Select Cabernet Sauvignon
$^1/_4$ cup butter
1 cinnamon stick

1. Combine sugar, Cabernet, butter, and cinnamon in a saucepan.
2. Heat on low to medium until sugar is dissolved and butter is melted. Add prepared pears. Simmer 20 minutes.
3. Remove pears to a container. Reduce the remaining liquid to desired consistency. Serve pears topped with Cabernet reduction.

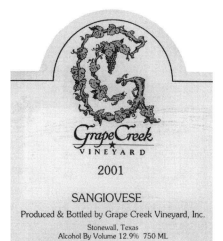

2001

SANGIOVESE

Produced & Bottled by Grape Creek Vineyard, Inc.

Stonewall, Texas
Alcohol By Volume 12.9% 750 ML

Grape Creek Vineyard, Inc.
Stonewall, Texas

If you go . . .
Grape Creek Vineyard, Inc.
P.O. Box 102
Stonewall, TX 78671
Phone: (830) 644-2710
Website: www.grapecreek.com
Hours:
Monday–Saturday: 10 a.m.–5 p.m.
Sunday: Noon–5 p.m.

The Inn on Grape Creek
Bed & Breakfast
Reservations: (800) 950-7392

Selected Wines
Sauvignon Blanc
Fumé Blanc
Riesling
Chenin Blanc
Cuvée Blanc (Chardonnay, Semillon,
  Sauvignon Blanc,
  Gewürztraminer blend)
Sangiovese
Merlot
Cabernet Trois (Cabernet Sauvignon,
  Ruby Cabernet, Cabernet Franc
  blend)
Holiday Rouge (Cabernet Sauvignon,
  Sangiovese blend)
White Zinfandel
Cabernet Blanc
Muscat Canelli

The Simes family enjoyed French-style dry wines years before they opened Grape Creek Vineyards. With consulting help from Dr. Enrique Ferro, who has a background in oenology, the family's dreams took shape.

Located only ten minutes from historic downtown Fredericksburg and about an hour from either Austin or San Antonio, Grape Creek Vineyard's warm days and cool evenings are conducive to growing grapes. The first planting, in 1985, covered six acres. By 1987, the vineyard carpeted a total of seventeen acres. Grape Creek's entire expanse of land covers 100 acres and includes a five-acre peach orchard, an herb garden, a blackberry patch, and picnic grounds on South Grape Creek (origin of the vineyard's name).

The winery's first wines were released in 1989. Its Chardonnay immediately began collecting awards.

Grape Creek Vineyard is active in a number of Texas wine events. Guests are invited out to enjoy a picnic by the creek or stay overnight in the Inn on Grape Creek bed and breakfast, located above the tasting room. Amenities in the Bluebonnet Room and the Grape Room include a complimentary bottle of wine, delicious continental breakfast, full kitchen, private bath, and beautiful view of the vineyard.

Grape Creek Vineyard offers two recipes provided by Carolyn, the lovely wife of long-time assistant winemaker Troy Rose.

Carolyn's Veal Parmesan over a Bed of Angel Hair Pasta

Serves 2

The ingredients for this delicious entrée can be adjusted for different quantities. You won't believe how incredibly easy this dish is to prepare.

$^1/_4$ cup Italian bread crumbs

$^1/_4$ cup grated Parmesan

$^1/_2$ teaspoon salt

$^1/_2$ teaspoon paprika

Dash of pepper

2 teaspoons garlic powder

3–5 veal loin chops, $^1/_2$ to $^3/_4$ inch thick (Ask your butcher to tenderize.)

2 eggs, beaten

$1^1/_2$ cups olive oil

3–5 slices mozzarella cheese

1 teaspoon oregano

One 12-ounce package angel hair pasta

$^1/_4$ cup Grape Creek Vineyard red wine (Sangiovese is incredible.)

26 ounces of your favorite pasta sauce (Marinara really makes a marvelous difference.)

1. Mix first five ingredients plus 1 teaspoon garlic powder. Set aside.

2. Heat pasta sauce in separate pot with the red wine and second teaspoon garlic powder.

3. Preheat oven to 350°F.

4. Dip chops in eggs, then in crumb mixture. Brown on both sides in $1^1/_2$ cups hot olive oil (as in deep fryer; this holds the egg and crumb mixture together).

5. Pour $1^1/_2$ cups of the seasoned pasta sauce in a separate skillet (or baking dish); set aside the rest of the sauce.

6. After chops are browned, place in the skillet (or baking dish) with the $1^1/_2$ cups pasta sauce.

7. Place a slice of mozzarella cheese on each chop. Sprinkle with oregano.

8. Cover; simmer or bake for 50 minutes, or until meat is done.

9. About 15 minutes before chops are done, start boiling water for the pasta and heat the remaining seasoned sauce.

10. Place pasta, then veal chops and all extra pasta sauce on each plate.

Wine: Serve with any Grape Creek Vineyard dry red wine.

 Pumpkin Cheesecake

Makes one 10-inch cheesecake

For Crust:

$^3/_4$ cup graham cracker crumbs
$^1/_4$ cup finely chopped pecans
$^1/_4$ cup finely chopped almonds
$^1/_4$ cup brown sugar, firmly packed
$^1/_4$ cup granulated sugar
$^1/_4$ cup unsalted butter, softened

1. Preheat oven to 350°F (325°F if using glass pan).
2. Use a rolling pin to smash pecans and almonds to a fine-grained substance.
3. Combine crumbs, pecans, almonds, sugars, and butter.
4. Press mixture into 10-inch pie pan. While preparing filling, freeze crust for approximately 30 minutes.

For Filling:
All dairy ingredients should be at room temperature.

1 cup canned, solid pumpkin

3 large eggs

1$\frac{1}{2}$ teaspoons ground cinnamon

1 tablespoon cornstarch

2 tablespoons condensed milk

1 tablespoon heavy cream

1 cup granulated sugar

$\frac{1}{2}$ teaspoon salt

$\frac{3}{4}$ teaspoon ginger

$\frac{3}{4}$ teaspoon nutmeg

1$\frac{1}{2}$ pounds cream cheese, softened

1$\frac{1}{2}$ teaspoons vanilla

1. In a bowl, whisk together pumpkin, eggs, cinnamon, salt, ginger, nutmeg, and $\frac{3}{4}$ cup sugar.

2. In another bowl with electric mixer, cream remaining ingredients together. Blend the two bowls together in one large bowl.

3. Pour filling into crust. Bake pumpkin cheesecake in preheated oven 40 to 50 minutes, or until the center is set.

4. Let cheesecake cool. Cover and refrigerate for 8 hours. Top with your favorite garnish.

Wine: Serve with Grape Creek Vineyard Muscat Canelli.

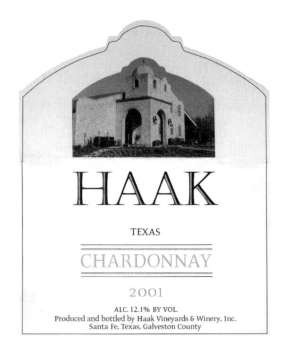

Haak Vineyards & Winery, Inc.
Santa Fe, Texas

If you go . . .
Haak Vineyards & Winery, Inc.
6310 Avenue T
Santa Fe, TX 77510
Phone: (409) 925-1401
Website: www.haakwine.com
Hours: Vary by season; private group tours available by appointment.
Summer (May–October):
Monday–Friday: 11 a.m.–6 p.m.
Saturday: 11 a.m.–7 p.m.
Sunday: Noon–6 p.m.
Winter (November–April; see Holidays.):
Monday–Friday: 11 a.m.–5 p.m.
Saturday: 11 a.m.–6 p.m.
Sunday: Noon–5 p.m.
Holidays:
Closed Easter Sunday, Thanksgiving Day, Christmas Day, and New Year's Day.
Group tours available. Call for information.

Selected Wines
Blanc du Bois
Chardonnay
Reserve Chardonnay
Sangiovese
Sauvignon Blanc
Syrah
"Reddy Vineyards" Cabernet Sauvignon
Zinfandel
Cabernet Sauvignon
Reserve Cabernet Sauvignon
Texas Ruby Port

Haak Vineyards & Winery, Inc., the first vineyard in Galveston County along the southern coast of Texas, grew from a gift. In 1975, when Gladys Haak presented her husband Raymond with two Concord grape vines, he planted an experimental vineyard next to the couple's home.

The Haaks' dream of running a winery was fulfilled when Haak Vineyards & Winery opened in 2001. Today, the vineyard boasts three acres of grapes and an 11,000-square-foot winery with a cellar located nine feet underground (a rare find in the coastal region). A sump pump keeps the water out of the cellar, which is used for aging and storing wines.

Gladys Haak, an accountant and marketing professional, has a background in agriculture (she grew up on a rice farm in Dickinson, Texas). Raymond is an electrical engineer and holds the patent on a spring-loaded thermometer popular in industrial settings.

The Santa Fe warm breezes and microclimate present favorable conditions for the vineyard. The Haaks grow two grape varieties: Blanc du Bois and Black Spanish, as well as two varieties of Mediterranean olives. Their wines have already won a number of prestigious awards.

Raymond and Gladys host various special events at their winery, such as "Haaktoberfest," the "Ole Time Thanksgiving Festival," and an oyster fry. A deli and picnic grounds provide amenities for guests. The winery's website has a complete list of events offered throughout the year.

Gladys Haak enjoys cooking, and here she shares three delightful recipes from the vineyard.

Creole Bouillabaisse

Serves 8

This is an elegant meal to serve to impress someone. —Gladys Haak

> 1 pound fresh fish fillets, cut in 1$\frac{1}{2}$-inch chunks
> $\frac{1}{2}$ pint fresh oysters
> 1 pound peeled, deveined shrimp
> $\frac{1}{2}$ cup margarine, butter, or cooking oil
> $\frac{1}{3}$ cup flour
> 1 cup onion, chopped
> $\frac{1}{2}$ cup celery, chopped
> 2 cloves garlic, minced
> Two 13-ounce cans chicken broth
> 1 large can (28 ounces) tomatoes, undrained, cut up
> $\frac{1}{2}$ cup dry white wine

2 tablespoons parsley, chopped
1 tablespoon lemon juice
1 bay leaf
$1/2$ teaspoon salt
$1/4$ teaspoon cayenne pepper

1. Melt margarine in a large boiler pot over medium heat.
2. To prepare roux: Slowly blend $1/3$ cup flour into $1/2$ cup melted margarine. Stir constantly until mixture is medium brown in color. Add onion, celery, and garlic. Continue stirring until vegetables are tender. Gradually stir in chicken broth. Add remaining ingredients, except seafood. Bring to a boil and then simmer 10 minutes.
3. Add seafood and simmer 5 minutes, or until all seafood is done.

Wine: Serve with Haak Sauvignon Blanc.

  Creole Gumbo

I can't tell you how many times I've made this. It feeds a lot of people. Serve it with rice. Step 1 is important to get the roux as brown as possible. Tastes even better the next day.—Gladys Haak

1 cup oil
1 cup flour
8 ribs celery, chopped
3 large onions, chopped
1 green pepper, chopped
2 cloves garlic, minced
$1/2$ cup parsley, chopped

2 quarts chicken stock
2 quarts water
$^1/_2$ cup Worcestershire sauce
Tabasco sauce, to taste
$^1/_2$ cup ketchup
1 ripe tomato, cut up
2 tablespoons salt
1 teaspoon monosodium glutamate (MSG)
4 slices bacon
1–2 bay leaves
$^1/_4$ teaspoon thyme
$^1/_4$ teaspoon rosemary
Red pepper flakes, to taste
1 pound okra, sliced
Your Choice: Shrimp, crabmeat, oysters, or chicken
1 teaspoon molasses *or* brown sugar
A small amount of lemon juice

1. Make roux: Brown oil and flour in skillet. Sauté in roux: celery, onions, green pepper, garlic, and parsley. Stir in chicken stock and water. Add Worcestershire sauce, Tabasco sauce to taste, ketchup, tomato, salt, MSG, bacon, 1 or 2 bay leaves, thyme, rosemary, and red pepper flakes. Simmer $2^1/_2$ to 3 hours.
2. Add okra and your choice of shrimp, crabmeat, oysters, or chicken. Add molasses or brown sugar, and a bit of lemon juice. Continue to cook another 30 minutes to 1 hour.
3. Remove gumbo from heat and let sit awhile to bring out the flavors even more. (This recipe tastes even better if refrigerated and reheated the next day.)

Wine: Serve with Haak Chardonnay.

Mom's Cottage Cheese Pie

Serves 6–8

I'm following up on my mother's Cottage Cheese Pie recipe. My sister, Judy Wright, sent me a recipe similar to my mom's recipe. I discussed it with the family and made a few recommended changes. I prepared it one Mother's Day, and my mom (Barbara Shead) gave me the taste-test approval that it tasted like hers. So . . . I am very happy to have a copy of one of my childhood favorites.

Of course, living on a farm in Santa Fe, Texas, in the 1950s and 1960s, we had many of the ingredients from the farm. We used milk from our own cows, made fresh cottage cheese, and gathered eggs from our chicken ranch! Owning a chicken ranch and egg farm, we were always looking for ways to use extra eggs.

For testing of the recipe, I used all commercial products and substituted low-fat versions to make it more heart healthy! In my next testing, I plan to use Splenda instead of sugar.—Gladys Haak

2 cups small-curd low-fat (2%) cottage cheese
3 eggs (or egg substitute)
2 teaspoons vanilla
$^1/_4$ teaspoon nutmeg
1 cup sugar
One 8-ounce can crushed pineapple, drained well
1 deep-dish pie shell, unbaked
$^1/_2$ teaspoon cinnamon

1. Preheat oven to 350°F.
2. Drain cottage cheese in colander.
3. In large mixing bowl, combine drained cottage cheese, eggs, and vanilla. Beat with electric mixer. Add nutmeg and sugar. Continue beating. Stir in pineapple.

4. Pour filling into unbaked pie shell, and sprinkle cinnamon on top.

5. Bake in preheated oven 45–60 minutes, or until knife inserted comes out clean.

Wine: Serve with Haak Blanc du Bois.

14

La Bodega Winery

Dallas/Fort Worth
International Airport,
Texas

If you go . . .

La Bodega Winery

Dallas/Fort Worth International
Airport
Terminal A, Gate 15
Dallas/Fort Worth International
Airport, TX 75261
Phone: (972) 574-6208 or (972) 574-
1440
Website: www.texaswinetrails.com/
bodega.htm
Hours: Open 365 days a year; times
may change with flight schedules.
Monday–Friday: 9 a.m.–9 p.m.
Saturday and Sunday: Noon–8 p.m.

Selected Wines

Private Reserve Merlot
Private Reserve Cabernet Sauvignon
Private Reserve Chardonnay
Texas Country Blush

Texas entrepreneurial spirit is known around the world. That's why it is no surprise that the first airport winery in the United States, and possibly the entire planet, just happens to be located at DFW Airport. Nestled alongside gift shops and newsstands, La Bodega Winery invites travelers from all parts of the globe to sample award-winning Texas wines between flights. Talk about innovation.

Who would ever think to house a winery in an airport? This jet-set phenomenon was the brainchild of Gina Puente-Brancato, who owns La Bodega with her husband John Brancato. And if you think this winery simply offers a tasting room and retail operation, think again. La Bodega actually produces a portion of its wines at the airport. Depending on the time of year, customers can look through a viewing window and observe a grape press and fermentation tanks in action. La Bodega bottles most of its wine outside the airport through co-op arrangements with other Texas wineries.

The winery began when the Puente family, who already owned several airport retail shops, decided to combine some of their unused retail space with an American Airlines closet adjacent to one of their businesses. Gina, who has had a hand in the family business since she was 12, came up with the concept of converting the space to an airport winery. La Bodega opened in 1995, and its popularity took off like a jet.

Prior to opening La Bodega, Gina earned a degree in broadcast journalism. Determined to pursue a retail career, she turned down an offer to anchor a news program. After a stint at Gap Kids/Baby Gap, Gina helped her father manage the family's three newsstand/gift shops at DFW Airport while her husband John had a successful business career that included key posts at Frito Lay. When the entrepreneurs opened La Bodega, news of an airport winery spread around the world and garnered widespread media attention.

La Bodega offers a wide selection of wines and other amenities at its shop. In addition to selling its own wines, the attractively appointed store features wines from many other Texas vineyards and wineries. It also offers an array of food and wine-related gifts, personalized wine labels, gift baskets, premium cigars and accessories, and—on select days—gourmet food tastings. The name *La Bodega,* which means "wine cellar" in Spanish, was inspired by Father Garcia de San Francisco y Zuñiga, who in 1659 established Texas's first vineyard and winery. (His image appears on the La Bodega label.)

La Bodega has received accolades for its innovative concept. *USA Today* featured La Bodega in its business travel section during the winery's first month of operation in 1995. In 1998, the Airport Council International–North America named La Bodega "Most Innovative Business at an Airport," and in 1999 the winery received the coveted "Diamond Award" from *On Board Magazine.* In 2000, *InStyle* magazine listed La Bodega Winery as a "Choice Stop" for DFW Airport travelers.

In addition to receiving honors for its business success and innovation, La Bodega's wines have won a number of prestigious awards. If you can't make it to DFW Airport, the La Bodega wines are also available at several Dallas/Fort Worth area retail shops.

Gina and her husband John are active in the Texas wine industry, where Gina assumed presidency of the Texas Wine and Grape Growers Association (TWGGA) in 2003. John uses his budgetary expertise to offer financial counsel to the organization. Together, Gina and John serve as ambassadors of Texas wine, introducing travelers from around the world to the delightful wines made in the Lone Star State. Next time I have time to spare between flights at DFW Airport, I know where I'll be heading.

In the meantime, Gina and John share this flavorful recipe for a classic chicken dish in a delicately flavored wine sauce.

La Bodega Chicken with Wine Sauce

Serves 2

Two 8-ounce boneless, skinless chicken breasts
4 tablespoons butter, divided, room temperature
1 1/2 tablespoons flour
2–3 tablespoons olive oil
1/2 cup La Bodega Private Reserve Chardonnay
1/3 cup fresh lemon juice
1/3 cup chicken stock
1/3 cup drained capers
1/3 cup fresh, chopped parsley
1/2 cup flour, for dredging chicken breasts
Salt and pepper

1. Pound 2 chicken breasts flat, to 1/4-inch thickness. Spread drained capers onto paper towel to remove excess liquid. Chop parsley. Set aside.
2. Squeeze fresh lemon juice. Set aside.
3. Combine 1/2 cup flour, salt, and pepper on dinner plate. Dredge chicken breasts in this mixture until lightly coated on both sides. Shake off excess flour.
4. Heat 2–3 tablespoons olive oil in heavy skillet. Cook chicken over medium-high heat until lightly golden on both sides (about 4–5 minutes per side). Move chicken to plate and keep warm.
5. Mix 1 tablespoon room-temperature butter with 1 1/2 tablespoons flour until smooth. Set aside.
6. Combine La Bodega Private Reserve Chardonnay, lemon juice, and chicken stock in skillet. Bring to boil over medium heat. Whisk in butter and flour mixture. Sauce

will thicken in 1–2 minutes. Stir in drained capers, fresh-chopped parsley, and 2–3 tablespoons room-temperature butter. Season with salt and pepper to taste. Pour sauce over chicken.

Tip: If sauce becomes too thick, gradually add more chicken stock.

Wine: Serve with La Bodega Private Reserve Chardonnay.

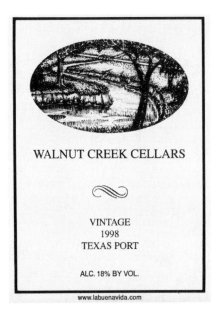

15

WALNUT CREEK CELLARS

VINTAGE
1998
TEXAS PORT

ALC. 18% BY VOL.

www.labuenavida.com

La Buena Vida Vineyards

Grapevine, Texas, and
Springtown, Texas

If you go . . .
La Buena Vida Vineyards at Grapevine
416 E. College Street
Grapevine, TX 76051
Phone: (817) 481-WINE (9463)
Website: www.labuenavida.com
Hours:
Monday–Saturday: 10 a.m.–5 p.m.
Sunday: Noon–5 p.m.

If you go . . .
La Buena Vida Vineyards at Springtown
650 Vineyard Lane
Springtown, TX 76082
Phone: (817) 220-4366
Website: www.labuenavida.com
Tours available by appointment only.

Selected Wines

Springtown Red
Springtown Merlot
Springtown Cabernet Sauvignon
La Buena Vida Central Valley Merlot
Grapevine La Dulce Vida (Cabernet
    Sauvignon, Ruby Cabernet,
    Merlot blend)
Springtown Mist (blush)
Springtown Merlot l'elegance
Springtown Chardonnay

Springtown Muscat Canelli
La Buena Vida Chardonnay
Walnut Creek Cellars Port
Springtown Muscat Dulce
Smith Estate Blanc de Blancs Brut
    (champagne)
Smith Estate Blanc de Blancs Ultra
    Brut (champagne)
Texmas Blush
Scarborough Mead

A visit to La Buena Vida in Grapevine, Texas, offers a glimpse into the winemaking days of years past. A museum adjacent to the tasting room houses artifacts collected by La Buena Vida's physician owner, Dr. Bobby Smith. Shelves display ancient tools from Dr. Smith's personal collection, such as a grape crusher–destemmer circa 1869, a collection of stave axes used to form the sides of a barrel, and an old-fashioned cheese slicer.

In Spanish, *La Buena Vida* means "the good life," and that remains the philosophy behind the vineyard's wines. The vineyard goes back to the 1970s, when Dr. Smith first planted its grapes, which were harvested in 1975. He was familiar with the art and science of grape growing; his father was a grape grower. The winery now produces its award-winning wines under a variety of labels including Springtown, La Buena Vida, Grapevine, Walnut Creek (named for the creek that winds through the vineyard), and Smith Estate (Champagnes). Two specialty wines include Texmas Blush (a light, semisweet Christmas blush) and Scarborough Mead (honey wine). Both are available year-round.

The general manager of marketing and sales for La Buena Vida, Camille McBee, operates an active schedule of special events that bring people out to either the Grapevine or Spring-town location to enjoy the good life. Camille, who has worked with La Buena Vida for nearly two decades, plans its events—which include weddings, corporate gatherings, private wine tastings, birthday and anniversary parties, and other gala cele-brations. She also teaches a variety of food and wine classes and seminars, writes a magazine wine column, and plays an active role in the Texas Wine and Grape Growers Association (TWGGA).

A fragrant herb garden sits just outside the tasting room in Grapevine. Picnic tables and shaded seating allow guests to relax and visit while touring La Buena Vida. The winery is also active in several local and statewide wine events.

In addition to the wines sold in the retail shop, Camille has stocked the area with a number of unique gift items including jewelry, gift baskets, crystal, wine-related gadgets and serving ware, and even baby gifts. I couldn't resist purchasing a "Vintage 2002" infant T-shirt for my newborn niece when I visited the winery.

Camille graciously granted me permission to include one of her original recipes, Camille's Ported Pears, in this cookbook.

Camille's Ported Pears

Serves 4-6

Camille McBee created this recipe as an ideal first course served with a lighter-style Port or as an accompaniment to venison or game birds. Camille, a Dallas native, is a third-generation Texan and general manager and marketing director for La Buena Vida Vineyards. The recipe has appeared in Anne Willan's Cooking With Wine *(Harry N. Abrams, 2001), a publication of COPIA—the American Center for*

Wine, Food & the Arts. Camille is a Master Lady of the Vine in the Order of the Knights of the Vine, past president of the Texas Wine & Grape Growers Association, member of the American Vintners Association, a charter member of Women for WineSense, and a member of COPIA in Napa, California. Her recipes and articles on wine and food pairing have been published in numerous wine publications. Camille is a graduate of Food & Wine Dynamics at the Culinary Institute of America (CIA) in St. Helena, California.

3 large Bartlett or Bosc pears
$^1/_2$ cup pear nectar
$^1/_2$ cup Walnut Creek Cellars Vida del Sol Port
1 tablespoon brown sugar
1 teaspoon ground cinnamon
Juice from 1 lemon
$^1/_2$ cup English Stilton or other bleu cheese
$^1/_2$ cup coarsely chopped walnuts

1. Preheat oven to 350°F.
2. Coat bottom of 9 x 13 glass baking dish with nonstick spray.
3. Halve pears, scooping out cores and stems, but leaving the peel. Cut a thin slice from the rounded side of pears so they sit flat, core side up. Place in baking dish.
4. Mix pear nectar with half of the Port and pour it over the pears.
5. Stir together sugar, cinnamon, and lemon juice. Sprinkle over pears.
6. Bake in preheated oven 10 minutes.
7. Crumble cheese into a bowl. Stir in walnuts, and spoon this mixture into the hollows of the pears, mounding it well. Moisten with remaining Port and continue baking until

pears are tender and cheese is brown, 20–30 minutes. Baste often so the Port and nectar mixture glazes the pears and forms a small amount of light sauce.

8. After baking, pour leftover sauce into a saucepan. Boil until reduced and slightly thickened.

Serving Suggestion: Serve pears warm over a bed of field greens with reduced sauce. Warm poppy-seed dressing may also be used as a dressing.

Wine: Serve with Walnut Creek Cellars Vida del Sol (a lighter-style Port).

16

LightCatcher Winery
Fort Worth, Texas

If you go . . .
LightCatcher Winery
6925 Confederate Park Road
Fort Worth, TX 76135
Phone: (817) 237-2626
Website: www.lightcatcher.com
Hours:
Friday, Saturday, Sunday: Noon–5 p.m.
Other times by appointment.

Selected Wines
LightCatcher Merlot
LightCatcher Cabernet Sauvignon
Texas Roads Chardonnay
Texas Roads Merlot
Texas Roads Cabernet Sauvignon
Strawberry Kiss Nouveau Merlot (Rosé)

Proprietors Caris and Terry Turpen created LightCatcher Winery to make small batches of high-quality wines. In essence, they have taken an artisan approach to the art and science of winemaking.

Caris Palm Turpen, an artist herself, is LightCatcher's winemaker. A highly regarded Emmy award–winning filmmaker, Caris notices the similarities between winemaking and filmmaking: both are a creative blend of art and science. Winemaking is not new to her family. Her mother's ancestry, of Greek heritage, includes generations of female winemakers. In addition to her family historical ties to winemaking, Caris has taken years of formal classes in oenology. While the Turpens do have a small vineyard adjacent to the winery, they purchase most of their fruit from reputable growers.

Terry Turpen brings a sense of pragmatism, coupled with humor, to LightCatcher—useful traits when dealing with the complexities of wines. The healthy mix of creative energy and solid wine knowledge is reflected in LightCatcher's wines, which have already begun to collect awards.

It is no surprise that this creative couple incorporates their appreciation for art into their work with wines. Art is displayed on the winery's label, at the winery itself through its art gallery and gift selection, in the fabulous stemware collection available for purchase, and in the gift baskets that feature accessories such as a hammered stainless steel spoon or earthenware pot. The website offers visual images of these beautiful, well-crafted items. The stemware collection is exceptional.

Caris and Terry host special events in and out of the winery, including a "Grand Release Ceremony" in the fall, a jazz concert, and a number of holiday gift drives/wine tasting parties throughout the holiday season. They also host private wine tasting parties at the winery or in area homes or businesses. Their website offers detailed descriptions of the special events and beautiful photos of the gift baskets and stemware available for purchase.

Caris graciously shares three recipes, which reflect her creative flair.

 ## Halibut with Shrimp Sauce chez LightCatcher

Serves 4

Caris and Terry enjoy this flavorful dish with a Greek salad or sautéed zucchini.

4 halibut steaks
Juice of 1 lemon
1 medium yellow onion, finely chopped
2 celery ribs, finely chopped
2 tablespoons parsley, finely chopped
3 garlic cloves, finely minced
One 15-ounce can diced tomatoes, juice included
1 cup béchamel sauce (see recipe)
$1/2$ cup Texas Kiss Rosé
$1/4$ pound small or bay shrimp
1 teaspoon dried Greek (not Mexican) oregano
2 tablespoons butter
Salt and pepper, to taste
Flour, for dusting halibut

For Béchamel Sauce:

2 tablespoons butter
2 tablespoons flour
1 cup milk
Salt and pepper, to taste

1. Melt 2 tablespoons butter over medium heat on top of the stove.
2. Add 2 tablespoons flour. Stir until blended.
3. Gradually add 1 cup of milk that has been slightly heated. Season with salt and white pepper to taste.
4. Simmer, stirring almost constantly, over low heat for about 5 minutes, or until mixture starts to boil and thickens. Makes 1 cup.

For Halibut with Shrimp Sauce:

1. Preheat oven to 375°F.
2. Wipe halibut steaks. Season with salt and pepper, and dust lightly with flour. Gently brown the fish on both sides in butter. Remove from pan; pour lemon juice over halibut. Set aside.
3. In a clean skillet, sauté onion, celery, and parsley until onions are translucent.
4. Add garlic and sauté 1 minute or until garlic releases fragrance, but does not brown. Add tomatoes, béchamel sauce, wine, oregano, salt, and pepper. Stir and simmer about 8 minutes. Add shrimp. Simmer another 2 minutes.
5. Place halibut steaks in a baking dish or individual casseroles. Pour shrimp sauce over steaks. Bake in preheated oven for 20 minutes.

Wine: Enjoy the halibut with a well-chilled LightCatcher Texas Kiss Rosé.

Lamb Shanks chez LightCatcher

Serves 2

Enjoy this hearty entrée with a crisp green salad.

Lamb shanks, 2 large or 4 small
1 medium yellow onion, chopped
5 cloves garlic, minced
One 15-ounce can diced tomatoes
1 tablespoon sugar
1 cup dry red wine
One 14^1/$_2$-ounce can beef broth
1 cup orzo (rice-shaped pasta)
Olive oil
^{1}/$_2$ teaspoon dried oregano (adjust to your taste)
^{1}/$_2$ teaspoon dried rosemary (adjust to your taste)
Salt and pepper

1. Rinse and dry shanks. Rub with salt, pepper, and some of the garlic. Generously sop with olive oil. Let marinate 1 hour.
2. Preheat oven to 300°F.
3. Slowly sauté onion in olive oil until translucent, about 10 minutes. Push onions aside in skillet. Raise heat and brown the marinated shanks. Add remaining garlic during last minute of browning. Add tomatoes and sugar. Stir well. Add herbs and wine. Stir again. Cover pan.
4. Bake in preheated oven 45 minutes. Remove from oven.
5. Raise oven to 350°F. On stovetop, add broth to lamb mixture and bring to simmer. Add orzo and return to simmer.
6. Cover, return to oven for 30 minutes.

7. Remove lid and bake uncovered for another 15 minutes. Remove from oven. Let rest 10 minutes.

Wine: Serve with LightCatcher Texas Roads Merlot.

 ## Sweet Curry Chicken chez LightCatcher

Serves 2

When served with Texas Roads Chardonnay, the spices pop up the tropical fruit notes in the wine. This dish is delightful when accompanied by a salad of baby greens.

1 medium yellow onion, chopped
4 cloves garlic, minced
One 15-ounce can diced tomatoes, juice included
1 can coconut milk (not coconut cream), stirred to
    incorporate thick into thin
One 14^1/$_2$-ounce can chicken broth
2 tablespoons "sweet" curry powder (see Note)
1 teaspoon dried rosemary
1 tablespoon sugar
Salt and pepper
1 tablespoon olive oil
4 chicken thighs, skinned
1 cup Texmati or basmati rice

1. Preheat oven to 350°F.
2. Sauté onion in olive oil until transparent. Add garlic and sauté another 2 minutes. Add tomatoes, curry powder, coconut milk, chicken broth, rosemary, sugar, salt, and pepper. Stir thoroughly. Simmer, covered, 5 minutes.

3. Add rice. Stir to make sure rice is evenly distributed on bottom of pan. Place chicken thighs on top of mixture. Cover.

4. Bake in preheated oven 1 hour.

5. Remove from oven and let sit, covered, 10 minutes.

Note: "Sweet" curry is an Indonesian-style curry that is very light on chile powder. It is very flavorful, but not hot.

Wine: Serve with LightCatcher Texas Roads Chardonnay.

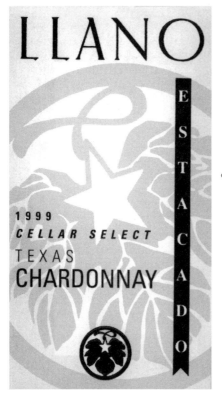

17

Llano Estacado Winery

Lubbock, Texas

If you go . . .
Llano Estacado Winery
P.O. Box 3487
Lubbock, TX 79452
Phone: (806) 745-2258
Website: www.llanowine.com
Hours:
Monday–Saturday: 10 a.m.–5 p.m.
Sunday: Noon–5 p.m.

Selected Wines
Cabernet Sauvignon
Cabernet Sauvignon Cellar Select
Merlot
Merlot Cellar Select
Chenin Blanc
Chardonnay
Chardonnay Cellar Select
Sauvignon Blanc
Johannisberg Riesling
Port
Signature Red
Signature White
Llano Blush

The history of Llano Estacado Winery stretches back to its founding in 1976. Today, Llano (pronounced "YAH-no") is one of the largest wineries in the state, producing many award-winning wines. It was here that I discovered one of my favorite food and wine combinations.

The winery tour takes guests through the entire winemaking process. White wines ferment in a huge area stacked with oak barrels and filled with a glorious aroma. The red wine room contains barrels where the reds age from ten to twenty-two months, except for one wine that stays in the barrel for about three years (more on this later). It was at this point of the tour—as we absorbed the delightful wine aroma wafting through the cellar air—that our guide mentioned the combination of Port and vanilla ice cream. I hadn't eaten lunch yet, so my ears perked up particularly high when he mentioned the blend of creamy, pure vanilla ice cream drizzled with Port wine. The blissful blend danced in my mind. When I finally had the opportunity to try this magical blend, I was delighted. To the tour guide at Llano Estacado, thank you for expanding my dessert repertoire.

Getting back to the winery, Llano has a blush room in addition to the red and white rooms. Texans seem to like chilled blush wines, which are especially popular at weddings in the Lone Star State. Visitors pass a window looking into the bottling room. An educational feature is the display of barrels that have been cut open, allowing a peek inside.

Llano Estacado has a small vineyard adjacent to the winery, and the owners purchase some of their grapes from other reputable growers in the area. Three grape varieties are grown on-site: Nebbiolo, Sangiovese, and Viognier. The winery is located in an ideal grape-growing region, where the 3,200-foot elevation provides warm days and cool nights.

The winery has a large tasting room and retail shop offering a huge selection of wine accessories and gift items, cookbooks, gift baskets, Llano Estacado brand gourmet food products, and of course the wines. The shop also features a wide selection of Llano Estacado Port wines, handsomely bottled in distinctive decanters (designed to enjoy alone or drizzled over your favorite vanilla ice cream). As for the wine aged three years in the barrel, it is called Viviano and is displayed and sold in the shop. The name "Viviano" is a combination of the name of a former Llano Estacado executive's wife (Vivian) and the Spanish word *llano* (a grassy plain). The wine is an award-winning blend of Cabernet Sauvignon, Cabernet Franc, Sangiovese, and Merlot.

Llano Estacado hosts various special events throughout the year, including a charity fund-raiser called "Chocolate Fantasia." The winery teams up with the South Plains Chefs Association and hosts a chocolate competition featuring chefs of all levels, ranging from amateur to professional. Competitors prepare phenomenal, breathtaking chocolate desserts, which guests have the pleasure of devouring. Another event, "Clay Days," is a summertime pottery fest featuring artists from Lubbock and around the state. Wines are sold by the glass, and guests have a chance to purchase unique pieces of pottery and art. Throughout the year, Llano Estacado holds several chocolate tastings and wine and cheese seminars. The website offers a comprehensive list of events and programs.

One visit to Llano Estacado Winery is all it takes to realize the staff's appreciation for the beauty of wine and food. Tasting room director Russell Gillentine graciously shares the following five recipes. The Deviled Crab was developed by Walter Haimann. Trenette al Pesto, Patate alla Salsiccia, and Caponata were created by Greg Bruni. Food consultant Bill Delassandro developed the Mesa Salmon.

 ## Deviled Crab

Serves 6

Serve as a flavorful first course or delightful luncheon entrée.

Ingredients

> 3–4 cans crabmeat or 1 to 1¹/₂ pounds fresh crabmeat
> ¹/₂ cup celery, very finely chopped
> ¹/₄ cup onion, very finely chopped
> Olive oil (to sauté celery and onions)
> ¹/₄ cup Llano Estacado Sauvignon Blanc
> 1 cup bread crumbs

Second set of ingredients:

$^1/_2$ can cream of mushroom soup
$^1/_2$ teaspoon salt
$^1/_4$ teaspoon pepper
$^1/_2$ teaspoon garlic powder
1 teaspoon Worcestershire sauce
6–8 drops hot pepper sauce
1 cup heavy cream
1 tablespoon fresh lemon juice

1. Preheat oven to 350°F.
2. Sauté celery and onion in olive oil until limp. Add wine. Simmer 5 minutes.
3. Mix soup, spices, and the rest of the second set of ingredients. Add to the sautéed mixture. Heat until it just begins to boil. Add crabmeat and bread crumbs.
4. Place in individual casserole dishes. Top with additional bread crumbs.
5. Bake in preheated oven until bubbly throughout.

Wine: Serve with Llano Estacado Sauvignon Blanc or Llano Estacado Signature Wine.

Trenette al Pesto (Fine Ribbon Noodles with Pesto)

Serves 4

1 cup fresh basil leaves, tightly packed
2 tablespoons pine nuts
3 garlic cloves, peeled
Salt
3 tablespoons grated Pecorino cheese
3 tablespoons freshly grated Parmesan
$^1/_2$ cup extra virgin olive oil
2 medium boiling potatoes
1 pound green beans, trimmed
13 ounces trenette noodles

1. Wash the basil leaves and dry them well.
2. Combine pine nuts, garlic, and basil in blender. Add a little salt, the cheeses, and a small amount of the oil. Puree the mixture. Pour in remaining oil. Blend for 1–2 seconds. Set aside.
3. Peel potatoes and cut into julienne strips.
4. Bring a large saucepan of water to boil. Drop in beans and cook 5 minutes. Add potatoes and cook 2 minutes. Add noodles.
5. When noodles are cooked al dente, about 5 minutes, drain mixture and turn out onto a serving plate.
6. Toss with the prepared pesto and serve.

Wine: Serve with Llano Estacado Sauvignon Blanc or Llano Estacado Cabernet Sauvignon.

Mesa Salmon

Serves 4

For Salmon:

4 salmon steaks
1 cup Llano Estacado Chardonnay
1 small lime

1. Place salmon steaks in shallow pan. Squeeze lime juice over steaks. Pour wine over steaks. Lightly season with your favorite fish seasonings. Cover and refrigerate 1 hour. Make Fresh Fruit Salsa while salmon is chilling.
2. Remove from refrigerator and grill for approximately 3 minutes on each side.

For Fresh Fruit Salsa:

1 medium cantaloupe, peeled and seeded, chopped into
    bite-sized pieces
1 lemon
2 limes
¼ cup Llano Estacado Chardonnay
2 jalapeño peppers, seeded, diced
¼ cup fresh cilantro

1. Combine cantaloupe and peppers. Set aside.
2. Combine lemon and lime juices with wine. Mix well. Add cilantro and let sit 10 minutes.
3. Pour the juice mixture over the cantaloupe and peppers.

Toss well. Refrigerate 1 hour. Serve chilled over grilled salmon steaks.

Wine: Serve with Llano Estacado Chardonnay.

 ## Caponata

Serves 2

1 eggplant, washed and cut into $1/2$-inch cubes
1 tablespoon salt
$1/4$ cup olive oil
$1/2$ to 1 onion, roughly chopped
2 red peppers (or 1 red, 1 green)
2 ribs celery, sliced
One 16-ounce can peeled tomatoes, cut into chunks, liquid
    reserved
2 tablespoons wine vinegar
1 clove garlic, crushed
One 4-ounce can sliced olives
1 tablespoon capers
Salt and pepper, to taste

1. Sprinkle eggplant cubes with salt. Mix well and let drain in colander 1 hour. Rinse under running water and pat dry.
2. Heat oil in large pan; add onion, peppers, and celery. Cook over moderate heat 5 minutes, stirring. Add eggplant and cook another 5 minutes, stirring. Add tomatoes and liquid from tomatoes, vinegar, and crushed garlic. Cook 2 minutes, stirring. Add sliced olives and capers. Stir well.
3. Simmer, uncovered, over moderate heat 15 minutes or

until most of the liquid has evaporated. Season with salt and pepper.

Wine: Serve with a full-bodied red wine, such as Llano Estacado Cabernet Sauvignon or Merlot.

 Patate alla Salsiccia (Potato with Spicy Italian Sausage)

Serves 6

7 ounces spicy Italian sausage
3 tablespoons extra virgin olive oil
1 onion, chopped
6 large baking potatoes, peeled and sliced
Salt and freshly ground pepper

1. Remove skin from sausage and break up the meat.
2. Heat oil in a large cast-iron skillet. Add sausage, onion, and potatoes. Cook, covered, over low heat 30 minutes.
3. Uncover and increase heat. Sauté, stirring constantly, until potatoes are brown. Season with salt and pepper, and serve.

Wine: Serve with Llano Estacado Sauvignon Blanc, Merlot, or Cabernet Franc.

18

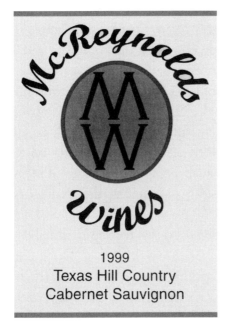

1999
Texas Hill Country
Cabernet Sauvignon

McReynolds
Wines

Cypress Mills, Texas

If you go . . .
McReynolds Wines
706 Shovel Mountain Road
Cypress Mills, TX 78654
Phone: (830) 825-3544
Website: www.mcreynoldswines.com
Hours:
Saturday: 10 a.m.–6 p.m.
Sunday: Noon–6 p.m.
Other times by appointment.

Selected Wines
Chenin Blanc
Sauvignon Blanc
Rose of Chenin
Cabernet Sauvignon
Merlot
Ruby Cabernet

Mac and Maureen McReynolds grew familiar with the wine industry while living in northern California in the 1970s. When they weren't working at their Stanford University research posts, they spent time visiting nearby wineries. Intrigued with the industry, they each took part-time jobs at two different California wineries, eventually teaming up with friends to grow grapes and make wines on an amateur basis.

When the couple returned to Austin, they became active in the Texas Wine and Grape Growers Association, and in 1989 purchased five acres of Hill Country land forty miles west of the city. The sprawling stretch of land included a structure that once served as a winery, and the couple continued to make wines on an amateur, rather than full-time commercial, basis. They switched gears from hobbyists to professionals when their wines began winning awards. McReynolds Winery opened in 2000, and the couple began selling their wines to the public.

The Brown Bomber, the official guest-greeting Chihuahua, cheerfully welcomes visitors to McReynolds. Earl Grey, the winery cat, also keeps watch over the winery and vineyard. In addition to opening their winery to visitors, the couple participates in a number of wine events around the state. The McReynolds website has a list of activities.

The four-acre vineyard provides a portion of the grapes for McReynolds, and is supplemented by grapes that the couple purchases from other reputable vineyards.

Maureen McReynolds provided the recipe for this hearty dish, perfect for a cool Texas evening.

Eggplant and Tomato Pie

Serves 4

This recipe is flexible regarding quantities and proportions of vegetables used. Serve it with a crusty French or Italian bread and a green salad. It serves four hearty eaters as a main dish.—Maureen McReynolds

1 medium eggplant
2 or more ripe tomatoes
2 medium onions
2 green peppers
2 cloves garlic
$1/2$ cup grated Parmesan cheese
3 tablespoons olive oil, plus extra for cooking the eggplant
1 baked pie shell

1. Preheat oven to 350°F.
2. Slice thinly the eggplant, tomatoes, onions, and peppers. Lightly sauté eggplant slices.
3. Dice garlic finely, and mix with 3 tablespoons olive oil. Set aside.
4. Arrange sliced vegetables in layers in the baked pie shell, alternating eggplant, peppers, onions, and tomatoes. Sprinkle some of the Parmesan cheese and garlic-flavored olive oil over each layer of tomatoes before adding the next round of eggplant, peppers, onions, and tomatoes. Sprinkle any remaining olive oil and Parmesan cheese on top.
5. Bake in preheated oven about 30 minutes or until vegetables are soft and well cooked.

Wine: Serve with McReynolds Wines Cabernet Sauvignon or Merlot.

19

Messina Hof Winery & Resort
Bryan, Texas

If you go . . .

Messina Hof Winery & Resort

4545 Old Reliance Road
Bryan, TX 77808
Phone: (979) 778-9463
Toll-free: (800) 736-9463
Website: www.messinahof.com
Hours: Open seven days a week.
Retail room (wine and gift items)
Monday–Saturday 10 a.m.–7 p.m.
Sunday: Noon–4 p.m.
Tours: No reservations required.
Monday–Friday: 1:00 p.m., 2:30
p.m., and 5:30 p.m.
Saturday: 11:00 a.m., 12:30 p.m.,
2:30 p.m., 4:00 p.m., and 5:30 p.m.
Sunday: 12:30 p.m. and 2:30 p.m.
Website has information on tour fees.
Private tours available upon request
during regular hours of operation; 10-
person minimum. Tasting room and
gift shop closed on Christmas Day
and New Year's Day.
Vintage House Restaurant
Lunch:
Wednesday–Saturday: 11 a.m.–4 p.m.
Sunday: Noon–4 p.m.
Dinner:
Wednesday–Saturday: 5–10 p.m.
Sunday: 4–6 p.m.
Reservations/information: (979)
778-9463, ext. 34, or
vintage@messinahof.com
Vintage House Restaurant is closed
Christmas Day and New Year's Day
(private events may be scheduled).

The Villa Bed & Breakfast

Luxurious accommodations on the
winery property
Reservations/information: Call
(979) 778-9463, ext. 22 for
reservations. Check website for
photos, rates, and other information.
**The Ultimate Wine & Food Pairing
Cookbook II**
To order Merrill Bonarrigo's
cookbook, call Messina Hof at (979)
778-9463 or (800) 736-9463; or visit
the website at messinahof.com.

Selected Wines

Chardonnay
Sauvignon Blanc
Pinot Grigio
Sparkling Wine
Chenin Blanc
Riesling
Gewürztraminer
White Zinfandel
Pinot Noir
Cabernet Sauvignon
Merlot
Zinfandel
Shiraz
Port

Messina Hof is a marriage of talent, a marriage of two different ancestries, and a marriage of two very special people who offer a wide array of award-winning wines. Paul and Merrill Bonarrigo, Messina Hof's proud owners, planted their first grapes in 1977. The first vintage was bottled in 1983, but the story of Messina Hof dates back centuries.

If you are fortunate enough to meet Paul, chances are he will be wearing a distinctive red beret, a symbol of the Bonarrigo family's winemaking tradition. Paul is the sixth-generation "Paul Bonarrigo" in the line of Paulo Bonarrigos who have been making wine in Messina, Italy (Sicily), for over two centuries.

In the Bonarrigo family, the privilege of making wine isn't handed down easily; it is earned. At age 16, Bonarrigo men take part in a "red beret ceremony," a rite of passage. The ceremony culminates years of preparation, during which elder Bonarrigos impart their wine knowledge to their young boys.

During the ceremony, the younger Bonarrigo must pass a comprehensive verbal wine exam administered by the family elders. Paul Bonarrigo VI recalls accepting his red beret, as he told the group what being the family winemaker meant to him. (The red beret tradition continues; Paul and Merrill's son Paul VII earned his several years ago. In fact, Merrill sometimes sports her own attractive red hat. Today, the winery has a Red Beret Club, which I'll explain later.)

While Paul VI's ancestral roots are in Italy, he grew up in New York, and although he officially became the family winemaker, he studied physical therapy in college. After graduating, Paul joined the United States Navy and served during Vietnam. He was stationed in California, where he furthered his winemaking education through the viticulture program at the University of California in Davis. Paul first arrived on Texas soil when he joined a physical therapy group in Laredo. He relocated to Bryan when the group opened an office there.

In 1977 Paul met his match, a realtor named Merrill, when he listed his home with her. After a whirlwind romance that began in January 1977, the couple wed in May of the same year. Paul continued with his physical therapy practice while Merrill remained a realtor. Things were soon to change.

Shortly after the Bonarrigos married, a physical therapy client of Paul's approached him with an idea. As Paul helped ease the pain of the client's sprained ankle, the young man (a Texas A&M student working on a dissertation on the feasibility of growing grapes for wine in Texas) worked on Paul, trying to convince him to plant an experimental vineyard. Paul was intrigued.

At that time it was generally believed that grapes wouldn't grow in Texas.

Always ready to accept a challenge, Paul and Merrill planted about thirty or forty different types of grapes on their property. Each year they culled the vineyard, clearing out the grapes that didn't fare well under the Texas sun. Surprisingly, some grapes not only grew on the Texas soil, they flourished!

As it turned out, the Bonarrigos' soil was the perfect pH for a vineyard. What's more, the land sloped, making drainage ideal. Messina Hof was born (named for Messina, Italy, and Hof, Germany—the ancestral roots of Paul and Merrill).

Because of his strong Italian winemaking background, Paul was no stranger to winemaking. Almost immediately, he became sought after for advice to others attempting to grow grapes in Texas. He is a three-time president of the Texas Wine and Grape Growers Association (TWGGA) and serves as a resource for winegrowers around the world. Messina Hof has become one of the largest wine producers in the state. Merrill, at the same time, showed her flair for gourmet cuisine and her real estate abilities by developing Messina Hof into an elegant full-service resort.

Today, the resort offers year-round events for its visitors.

Those wishing to spend a few hours may tour the winery and take a look at the bottling line, crusher, barrels (there are over 700 on the property), and tasting room.

An eye-pleasing stop is the art gallery, located in the winery's banquet facility. Each spring, Paul and Merrill hold a wine-label design competition. In the fall prior to each year's competition, 150 artists are invited to submit a design based on the year's theme. A committee of judges (two from an arts council, one local artist, and Paul and Merrill) selects the top competitors, who then submit a work of art for the label. The winner's design is used on the Messina Hof private reserves label for one year. The art gallery features winning designs from past competitions.

Following the tour, visitors enter the tasting room, where they sample award-winning Messina Hof wines. The winery also boasts a delightful gift shop, offering unique wine-related items and gourmet food products made by the staff.

Lunch and dinner are served in the winery's Vintage House Restaurant. Italian opera music fills the background as guests enjoy continental cuisine.

Guests who wish to stay overnight find exquisite lodging at The Villa, a dream come true for Merrill. An on-site bed and breakfast that opened in 1999, The Villa is an elegant structure displaying classic Italian design. After a competition, two student architects at Texas A&M were chosen to design the building—one was the creative genius, and the other took an engineering approach. Ten rooms, each with a private bath, accommodate guests. Each is tastefully decorated according to its own historical theme. Guests enjoy an elegant breakfast in the morning and wine and cheese in the afternoons. Port wine truffles are a bedtime luxury. Merrill traveled the world in search of antiquities for The Villa. Shutter doors were flown in from Germany, and stained glass windows came from the Louvre Museum in Paris.

Paul and Merrill attract visitors to Messina Hof Winery & Resort throughout the year with special events, banquets, weddings, vintner's dinners, murder mystery dinners, wine and food pairing seminars, and much more. The couple enjoys any opportunity to entertain and educate their guests. Perhaps their grandest event is the annual grape stomp, which attracts a few thousand people and is held in July and August. At 9 a.m.—before it gets too hot—guests begin picking grapes. At 10:30, the group returns their grape-filled buckets, and the grape stomp begins. Each year, some guests dress up like Lucy and Ethel in the famous *I Love Lucy* episode, adding to the thrill of the stomp. Paul and Merrill and the group clap and sing as everyone gets a turn at stomping. Following the stomp, guests tour the winery and enjoy a sumptuous harvest lunch.

As the afternoon sun bakes the land, guests enjoy air-conditioned comfort as they attend wine classes. Later, the group feasts on a celebratory dinner prepared in true Bonarrigo style.

One program that appeals to fans of Messina Hof wines is its distinctive Red Beret Club. The program, which charges a fee for membership, offers wonderful discounts on wines, as well as at the gift shop, Vintage House Restaurant, and The Villa. Each member receives an official red beret and many other exciting benefits. Visit the website for more details.

Messina Hof makes a wide variety of award-winning wines (a complete list is available on its website). Their Papa Paulo Port deserves special mention because it contains no brandy (Paul believes that brandy dominates the flavor of many Ports). The Messina Hof Port uses no grape skins—the Lenoir grape flows red without skins—and is enjoyed by people who cannot tolerate red wines.

The Bonarrigos enjoy educating the public on how to pair wine with food. They have developed a food and wine pairing chart, and they hold classes on the topic. Merrill brings wine pairing into homes through her newest book, *The Ultimate Wine & Food Pairing Cookbook II,* published in 2002. Recipes are organized by type of wine—a unique and helpful approach. Each recipe offers clear instructions, advice on presentation, and a suggested wine pairing. Merrill provides a detailed overview on wine pairing, with a guide for certain foods (such as "Mask salty dishes with slightly sweet wines"). She also offers suggestions for "wine-challenging foods" as well as a list of types of wines that pair well with most foods. I highly recommend this cookbook by Merrill Bonarrigo as an addition to any kitchen, especially for those who enjoy cooking with wine or serving wine alongside a meal. The following recipes are reprinted from *The Ultimate Food & Wine Pairing Cookbook II,* with Merrill Bonarrigo's permission.

 ## Sun-Dried Tomato-Basil Soup

Serves 4

8 Roma tomatoes
1 red onion, diced
3 cloves garlic, minced
1 tablespoon olive oil
12 ounces tomato juice
6 fresh basil leaves (or more to taste), cut into thin strips
6 sun-dried tomatoes, diced
1 teaspoon salt
$1/4$ teaspoon white pepper
Hot pepper sauce, to taste

1. Drop Roma tomatoes into boiling water for about 20 seconds. Remove and place in bowl of cold water; peel and seed when cool.
2. In medium skillet, sauté onion and garlic in olive oil until soft.
3. Purée onion mixture, Roma tomatoes, and tomato juice in food processor or blender.
4. Combine puréed mixture with basil, sun-dried tomatoes, salt, and pepper in a medium saucepan. Heat thoroughly. Add hot pepper sauce to taste. Garnish with fresh basil leaf and serve.

Wine: The soup pairs nicely with Messina Hof Cabernet Sauvignon, or other red wines such as Messina Hof Merlot or Messina Hof Pinot Noir.

 ## Giovanni's Chicken Gorgonzola

Serves 4

This is a chicken dish served with a full-bodied red wine. The strength of flavor of the cheese balances the wine. Be sure to taste to make sure there is enough Gorgonzola in the sauce to make this combination work.—Merrill Bonarrigo

4 boneless, skinless chicken breasts, butterflied
1 cup seasoned bread crumbs
8 tablespoons cooked spinach
4 tablespoons Gorgonzola cheese, crumbled
Salt and pepper to taste
1 tablespoon olive oil

For Gorgonzola Cream Sauce:

$1/2$ cup Messina Hof Merlot
1 cup heavy cream
1 tablespoon Gorgonzola cheese

1. Pound chicken breasts to $1/4$–$1/2$ inch thick.
2. Mix spinach and 4 tablespoons Gorgonzola cheese. Evenly divide among the four breasts, spreading mixture over each breast. Roll chicken in jelly roll fashion, fastening with toothpicks.
3. Bread rolled chicken. Season with salt and pepper.
4. Sauté chicken until brown on all sides and interior cheese begins to melt. Set aside.
5. Deglaze pan with Merlot (listed as part of the cream sauce). Gradually add cream and cheese until smooth and creamy.
6. Return the rolled chicken to pan to warm.
7. Serve chicken sliced into pinwheels and fanned over plate. Drizzle with sauce.

Wine: Serve with Messina Hof Merlot.

Garden Chicken

Serves 1

Serve the chicken breast over an ice-cream scoop of wild rice and a side of vegetables.

One 6-ounce boneless, skinless chicken breast
1 ounce olive oil
6–7 slices of mushroom
1 teaspoon capers
1 teaspoon chopped garlic
3–4 quarters of artichoke heart
1 tablespoon diced tomatoes
1–2 ounces Messina Hof Chardonnay
1 tablespoon whole butter

1. Grill the chicken breast until done, and move to a plate to keep warm.
2. Heat oil in a sauté pan. Carefully add mushrooms, capers, garlic, and artichoke hearts. Add tomatoes and wine to deglaze the pan. Continue cooking until mixture is almost dry.
3. At the last minute before serving, swirl in the whole butter to make a sauce.

Wine: Serve with Messina Hof Chardonnay.

Roast Pork Tenderloin

Serves 6

¹/₂ cup Messina Hof Port
1¹/₂ cups Messina Hof White Sparkling Grape Juice
¹/₄ cup sugar
4 apples, peeled and cored
1 pork tenderloin roast, 3–4 pounds
1 cup Messina Hof Pinot Noir
¹/₄ teaspoon salt
Flour, for thickening
¹/₂ teaspoon pepper
Fresh mint

1. Preheat oven to 350°F.
2. Boil wine, grape juice, and sugar until they reach a syrup consistency. Put apples in syrup and cover. Boil gently, turning apples periodically. Cook until tender. Remove apples to a flat dish. Cover with syrup; chill.
3. Sear tenderloin on all sides in a hot cast-iron ovenproof skillet. When browned, remove roast from pan and pour off all but two tablespoons oil. Deglaze with Pinot Noir. Salt and pepper meat and return to pan.
4. Place pan with meat into preheated oven and finish cooking to desired doneness, approximately 20 minutes.
5. Remove meat from pan. Add enough flour to the sauce to thicken.
6. Cover bottom of the serving plate with sauce and decorate with white cream design, if desired.
7. Thinly slice the tenderloin and fan along edge of plate. Garnish with candied apple and fresh mint.

Wine: Serve with Messina Hof Pinot Noir.

Port 'n' Cream Sundae

Serves 4

8 scoops vanilla ice cream
4 ounces Messina Hof Papa Paulo Port, plus additional for
    garnish
12 tablespoons Messina Hof Port Chocolate Fudge
12 tablespoons whipped cream
4 Maraschino cherries with stems
Mint sprigs for garnish

1. Put 2 scoops of vanilla ice cream in each of four stemmed wine glasses. Drizzle 1 ounce of Port over the ice cream in each glass. It will form a pool around the bottom of the ice cream.
2. Melt fudge sauce in the microwave until you can easily spoon 2–3 tablespoons over the ice-cream scoops. Top with whipped cream and a cherry.
3. Garnish with mint sprigs and a light sprinkling of Port.

Variation on the Theme:

Port 'n' Cream Freeze

Put 2 scoops of vanilla ice cream in the blender with 1 ounce Papa Paulo Port and 3 tablespoons whipped cream. Blend until thick and smooth. Pour into glasses and serve.

Wine: Serve with Messina Hof Papa Paulo Port.

20

PHEASANT RIDGE

TEXAS
CABERNET SAUVIGNON
10th Anniversary
1989

PRODUCED & BOTTLED BY PHEASANT RIDGE WINERY, LUBBOCK, TEXAS ALC. 12.4% BY VOL.

Pheasant Ridge Winery

Lubbock, Texas

If you go . . .
Pheasant Ridge Winery
Route 3, Box 191
Lubbock, TX 79403
Phone: (806) 746-6033
Website:
www.pheasantridgewinery.com
Hours:
Friday and Saturday: 10 a.m.–5 p.m.
Sunday: Noon–5 p.m.
Other times by appointment.

Selected Wines
Cabernet Sauvignon
Merlot
Pinot Noir
Proprietor's Reserve
Barrel Fermented Chardonnay
Dry Chenin Blanc
Proprietor's White

Pheasant Ridge is located in the countryside on the outskirts of Lubbock, Texas. There, the Gipson family's winery creates award-winning wines.

Vines were first planted on this stretch of land in 1979; the first harvest was in 1983. Several years later Pheasant Ridge's Cabernet Sauvignon won its first gold medal at a California wine competition. The winery's philosophy that Pheasant Ridge red wines are "never rushed" is especially illustrated in its Cabernet Sauvignon, which is aged at least two years before bottling.

The vineyard contains more than sixty sprawling acres of these grape varieties: Chenin Blanc, Chardonnay, Semillon, Pinot Noir, Merlot, Cabernet Sauvignon, and Cabernet Franc. All grapes are handpicked, and wines are estate bottled.

Friendly winery cats Corky and Paws welcome guests to the tasting room, which opened in 2001. Visitors may stroll the vineyard area, sample the wines, and browse the gift shop, where the wines and unique gift items are sold.

During the tasting, the enthusiastic staff explains that Pheasant Ridge wines are "dry with a fruity finish." Food and wine pairings are discussed as the visitors start with the lightest wines and proceed to the most full-bodied selections.

The winery hosts a number of special events throughout the year, such as "Bar-B-Que and Cabernet," a picnic-style barbecue meal accompanied by a new-release Cabernet Sauvignon. Pheasant Ridge also participates in Texas wine events throughout the state.

During my visit, tasting room staff member Margaret McMillan explained that one of her favorite wine and food pairings is grilled pork loin with Pheasant Ridge Pinot Noir. She shares the recipe, with its unique southwestern twist.

Grilled Pork Loin

Serves 6

Margaret McMillan from Pheasant Ridge serves this bold and flavor-
ful pork loin with garlic mashed potatoes and grilled vegetables such
as zucchini and asparagus that have been lightly basted with olive oil.
She suggests adjusting the pork seasonings to your personal preference.

1 pork loin, about 3 pounds
3–4 tablespoons Dijon mustard
³/₄–1 cup sliced jalapeño peppers (can use the peppers from
   a jar)
6 ounces jalapeño/jack blend cheese, sliced
Salt and freshly ground pepper
¹/₂ pound bacon slices, uncooked (optional)
Smoke flavoring

1. Cut pork loin lengthwise, like you would slice a sub
sandwich roll. Do not cut completely through the roast.
2. Brush inside of tenderloin with Dijon mustard. Place
peppers on top of mustard. Top with cheese slices.
3. Close up the loin; seal with toothpicks. If using bacon,
wrap bacon slices around the closed loin and then seal with
toothpicks. Baste with a small amount of smoke flavoring
and season with salt and pepper. Let sit 30 minutes.
4. Grill over moderate flame for a total of 20–30 minutes,
depending on size of loin, until thoroughly cooked. Turn
loin frequently during cooking.

Wine: Serve with Pheasant Ridge Pinot Noir.

Pillar Bluff Vineyards

Lampasas, Texas

If you go . . .
Pillar Bluff Vineyards
300 Burnet County Road 111
Lampasas, TX 76550
Phone: (512) 556-4078
Website: www.pillarbluff.com
Hours:
Saturday: Noon–5 p.m.
Other times by appointment.

Selected Wines
White Merlot
Merlot
Cabernet Sauvignon
Estate Blush
Chenin Blanc
Chardonnay

Proprietors Peggy and Gill Bledsoe welcome visitors to one of the newest wineries in the state. Located in the northernmost section of the Texas Hill Country, Pillar Bluff's grapes benefit from the rich soils of Pillar Bluff Creek.

The Bledsoes' philosophy is reflected in the attention they devote to each bottle of Pillar Bluff wine. They believe that "truly memorable wines are those that gain complexity with time and judicious care." Their wines have already begun to collect prestigious awards.

Pillar Bluff Vineyards offers the following recipe as a lovely dip for a Valentine's Day party or a special gathering any time of year.

 ## Smoked Salmon Dip

Makes about 2 cups

One 8-ounce brick Philadelphia Cream Cheese
One 8-ounce container sour cream
¼ cup chopped onion
¼ teaspoon Worcestershire sauce
1 tablespoon capers
½ teaspoon garlic powder
6–8 ounces smoked salmon, flaked (bones removed)

1. Mix cream cheese and sour cream. Add remaining ingredients.
2. Chill several hours and serve.

22

Pleasant Hill Winery

Brenham, Texas

If you go . . .
Pleasant Hill Winery
1441 Salem Road
Brenham, TX 77833
Phone: (979) 830-VINE (8463)
Website:
www.pleasanthillwinery.com
Hours:
Saturday: 11 a.m.–6 p.m. (tours every
hour beginning at 11:30 until half
hour before closing)
Sunday: Noon–5 p.m. (tours every
hour beginning at 12:30 until half
hour before closing)
Group tours available during other
times by appointment.

Selected Wines
Tawny Rosso Forte (Port style)
Fumé Blanc
Rose (lighter than red, but not a
    Rosé)
Collina Rossa (red)
Collina Bianca
Chardonnay
Blanc du Bois (dessert wine)
Rosso Forte (dessert wine)

Bob and Jeanne Cottle's wine background began long before
Pleasant Hill Winery opened in 1997. Both had grandparents

who were winemakers; the old grape press handed down from Jeanne's grandfather is proudly displayed in Pleasant Hill's tasting room.

Pleasant Hill sits on about thirty gently sloping acres in the Brenham countryside. A beautiful church, visible from the winery, is featured on the Pleasant Hill wine labels.

Winery tours begin and end in the skillfully reconstructed barn situated on a hilltop overlooking the vineyard. Take a stroll through the vineyard and cool off in the cellar located on the lower floor of the barn. The cellar is the domain of Bob, who is an engineer. There, a lab stocked with meters, tubes, and other devices provide tools for conducting chemical analyses on the wines. These items serve as a reminder to visitors that winemaking is a science as well as an art. Bob and his tasting panel converge in the lab, tasting the wines periodically during their barrel-aging stage.

Upstairs, the tasting room is Jeanne's domain. In addition to the tasting bar featuring a full selection of Pleasant Hill wines, the area serves as the winery's gift shop. Jeanne, who is a teacher, brings creativity to the forefront in the well-stocked shop. Wine-related accessories, books, videos, housewares, and gourmet food items provide eye candy for shoppers in search of that perfect gift. Speaking of candy, the gift shop sells homemade chocolate truffles made with a Pleasant Hill dessert wine. On display in the tasting room is Bob's world-class collection of wine pulls.

Pleasant Hill hosts a number of special events throughout the year. In 2003, an event featuring guest artists was held to celebrate the winery's sixth anniversary. Later that year, the winery held a celebration marking the release of its Blanc du Bois, a sweet dessert wine. Blanc du Bois is attractively packaged in a blue bottle and pairs quite well with cheesecake, which was served at the event.

A very special event is Pleasant Hill's grape crush. The "Crush for Fun" weekends give adults and kids a chance to crush grapes, earn a T-shirt, and have a whole lot of fun. The website offers information on the winery's events.

Brenham offers something for everyone. In addition to winery tours, visitors get the scoop on ice cream when they tour Blue Bell Creameries (www.bluebell.com), visit a miniature horse farm, or enjoy a stroll through quaint downtown Brenham.

Long-term plans call for the addition of a bed and breakfast at the vineyard. In the meantime, The Outpost at Cedar Creek offers delightful bed-and-breakfast lodging in the countryside between Brenham and Round Top, Texas. The Outpost features a number of overnight selections. Choose from restored 100-year-old log cabins, a Mexican casita, a quaint cottage, or a room in the main house. Guests enjoy strolling around the Outpost's property, cozying up to a nighttime campfire, visiting the proprietor's library, and savoring a full-course homemade breakfast served in the rustic dining room. For more information, visit the website at www.outpostatcedarcreek.com.

Bob and Jeanne Cottle offer these two recipes from the vineyard, featuring lamb and pork roasts and flavorful blends of herbs and spices.

Spicy Braised Lamb Roast

Serves 8

6 garlic cloves, minced
1 tablespoon plus 1 teaspoon thyme leaves
1 tablespoon cumin seeds
2 teaspoons finely chopped rosemary
1 star anise
2 teaspoons fine sea salt
1 tablespoon coriander seeds
1 teaspoon coarsely ground white pepper
5-pound lamb roast, preferably from the hip section
$^{1}/_{4}$ cup extra virgin olive oil
3 cups Pleasant Hill Collina Bianca

1. Preheat oven to 300°F.
2. Combine garlic, spices, and other seasonings.
3. Cut slits in meat and rub spice mixture all over lamb, working it into the slits.
4. Heat oil in a medium roasting pan on top of the stove. Brown lamb on all sides over moderate heat. Add wine and cover pan.
5. Transfer roast to oven, cover, and braise the lamb in the oven for $2^{1}/_{2}$ hours, or until very tender. Baste as necessary to prevent it from drying out. Remove cover during the last $^{1}/_{2}$ hour to concentrate juices. Transfer lamb to carving board.
6. Strain the cooking juices through a fine sieve; skim the fat. Transfer juices to a gravy boat. Slice lamb and serve with juices.

Wine: Serve with Pleasant Hill Collina Bianca, which is made from the local Blanc du Bois grape.

 ## Thyme-Braised Pork Loin

Serves 8

3 tablespoons unsalted butter
10 garlic cloves, minced
2 carrots, finely chopped
2 medium onions, finely chopped
2 celery ribs, finely chopped
Sea salt and freshly ground pepper
5-pound untrimmed pork loin
2 teaspoons thyme leaves, plus 2 bunches thyme sprigs
1 star anise
¼ cup extra virgin olive oil
2–3 cups Pleasant Hill Collina Bianca

1. Preheat oven to 300°F.
2. Melt butter in large nonreactive metal roasting pan. Add garlic and onions; season with salt and pepper. Cook on stove over medium heat, stirring occasionally, until onions and garlic are softened but not browned, about 5 minutes.
3. Season the entire pork loin with salt, pepper, and thyme leaves. Heat oil in pan. Sear roast on stovetop over moderate heat until browned on all sides. Transfer pork to a platter and discard the fat in the pan; wipe the pan clean.
4. Place remaining vegetables and garlic and onions from step 2 in the bottom of the pan. Return pork to pan, placing

loin on top of vegetables. Add wine, bunches of thyme sprigs, and star anise. Bring to a boil on the stove.

5. Transfer casserole to the oven. Cover and braise pork, basting every 30 minutes, for about $2^1\!/_2$ hours, or until it is very tender. Remove the lid for the last $^1\!/_2$ hour to let juices concentrate.

6. Remove pan from oven. Carefully transfer meat to a carving board and season it to taste with salt and pepper. Cover loosely with foil and let stand for about 15 minutes. Strain the cooking juices through a fine sieve into a gravy boat. Thickly slice the pork and serve with the cooking juices.

Wine: Serve with Pleasant Hill Collina Bianca, which is made from the local Blanc du Bois grape.

23

Sister Creek Vineyards

Sisterdale, Texas

If you go . . .

Sister Creek Vineyards
1142 Sisterdale Road
Sisterdale, TX 78006
Phone: (830) 324-6704
Website:
www.sistercreekvineyards.com
Hours:
Sunday–Thursday: Noon–5 p.m.
Friday–Saturday: 11 a.m.–5 p.m.

Selected Wines
Chardonnay
Cabernet Sauvignon Blend
Pinot Noir
Merlot
Muscat Canelli

Sisterdale, population "about twenty-five," has the distinction of being the second-oldest town in the scenic Texas Hill Country. Its history dates back to the nineteenth century, when it was settled by a group of Germans who referred to themselves as the Latin Colonies. Research shows that vineyards were planted in the area as early as the 1860s.

Like the town where it is located, Sister Creek Winery has interesting historical roots. The winery, which opened in 1988, is located in a restored cotton gin that was used from 1885 until 1927.

Today, winemaker Danny Hernandez employs traditional European winemaking practices in the development of Sister Creek's award-winning French-style Burgundy and Bordeaux wines as well as its Italian Muscat Canelli.

Annette Mainz from Sister Creek Vineyards shares a recipe she developed using the winery's Muscat Canelli wine.

Roasted Muscat Pecans and Peach Topping

This recipe uses a full pound of pecans, so you'll have enough topping to keep some on hand in the freezer. Annette Mainz suggests serving this blissful blend of pecans and peaches atop vanilla ice cream when unexpected guests arrive.

For Pecans:

1 pound shelled pecans
Sister Creek Muscat Canelli, enough to cover pecans

1. Soak pecans in wine for about 30 minutes. Drain, reserving wine.
2. Preheat oven to 250°F.
3. Place pecans on cookie sheet in low oven. Roast for 1 hour.
4. After pecans are roasted, place in individual-sized bags and freeze.

For Peach Topping:

Fresh peaches, about 1 per person
Sister Creek Muscat Canelli

1. Peel and slice fresh peaches (as many as needed). Place in bowl.
2. Pour Sister Creek Muscat Canelli over the peaches to cover. (May use leftover wine from the Muscat pecans.)
3. Chill for a few hours before serving.

To serve:

1. Spoon chilled Peach Topping over vanilla ice cream.
2. Top with Roasted Muscat Pecans.

Wine: Serve with Sister Creek Muscat Canelli.

24

Spicewood Vineyards

Spicewood, Texas

If you go . . .
Spicewood Vineyards
1419 Burnet County Road
P.O. Box 248
Spicewood, TX 78669
Phone: (830) 693-5328
Website:
www.spicewoodvineyards.com
Hours:
Wednesday–Friday: Noon–5 p.m.
Saturday: 10 a.m.–5 p.m.
Sunday: Noon–5 p.m.

Selected Wines
Chardonnay
Chardonnay Dulce
Semillon
Semillon Reserve
Sauvignon Blanc
Cabernet Sauvignon
Cabernet Franc
Zinfandel
Merlot
Holiday Blush
Bluebonnet Blush (blend of
    Chardonnay and Cabernet
    Franc)
Medea (Cabernet Sauvignon, Merlot,
    Cabernet Franc, and Alicante
    Bouschet blend)
Cabernet Claret (Cabernet
    Sauvignon, Cabernet Franc, and
    Sauvignon Blanc blend)

In 1990, Madeleine and Edward Manigold founded Spicewood Vineyards with one goal in mind: to make the finest wines they could possibly produce. They opened the winery for commercial production in 1995, and since that time have won numerous awards and gained high respect from the Texas wine industry and beyond. The name is derived from the town of Spicewood, Texas, which is near Marble Falls and a short drive from either Austin or San Antonio.

The vineyard sits on a hillside, offering plenty of sun and drainage for growing grapes. Initially, one-and-a-half acres were planted in 1995. The vineyard now spans more than seventeen acres.

The original winery building is reminiscent of a nineteenth-century Hill Country home. When Spicewood Vineyards outgrew that building, it was converted to a storage area and replaced in 1999 by a two-story, 5,000-square-foot winery. The upper level serves as the setting for many special events held on the premises, everything from catered wine-release dinners to weddings and receptions. A covered pavilion overlooking the vineyard provides an area for outdoor entertaining.

The lower level of the building serves as the winemaking area, with tanks that have the capacity to ferment and store 10,000 gallons of wine.

Spicewood Vineyards maintains an active special events calendar. Madeleine and Edward host a number of celebratory gatherings and winemaker dinners at the winery, and they participate in many wine trail and statewide events and benefits. Artist shows, book signings, and other events attract visitors throughout the year. The gift shop features unique wine-related and jewelry items. Check their website for a comprehensive schedule of events, and for the opportunity to sign up for their wine lover's newsletter, which is distributed by e-mail.

Spicewood Vineyards wines have racked up numerous awards; its initial vintage Chardonnay was the winery's first award-winning wine. The wines are estate bottled.

Madeleine Manigold provides the recipe for hearty Beef Bourguignon, an ideal main course to savor on a cool Hill Country evening. Madeleine starts making it the day before, allowing it to marinate overnight. She adapted the recipe from "Mme. Imbert's Boeuf Bourguignon," which appeared in *Recipes from the French Wine Harvest*, by Rosi Hanson (Seven Dials, 2001).

Spicewood Vineyards Beef Bourguignon

Serves 6

We serve this dish during our annual Merlot Nouveau Celebration on November 1. It is extremely popular with our guests, and Spicewood Vineyards Merlot Nouveau, Estate, Texas Hill Country, is the perfect pairing for it.—Madeleine Manigold

2 pounds rump roast, cut into small cubes
$^1/_3$ pound thick-sliced hickory smoked bacon, cut into
    approximately 1-inch cubes
1 large onion
2 cloves
Bouquet garni of fresh thyme, parsley, bay leaf, and 2 cloves
    of garlic
1 bottle Spicewood Vineyards Merlot Nouveau (another
    Nouveau-style wine will do in a pinch)
Salt
6 black peppercorns
12 small onions
Olive oil
Beurre manié: 1 teaspoon room-temperature butter and 1
    teaspoon cornstarch

1. Prepare meat the day before in a marinade of wine, the peeled onion stuck with 2 cloves, bouquet garni, and the bacon, salt, and peppercorns.
2. The next day, drain meat, saving all of the marinade. Dry the meat, large onion, and bacon slices on paper towels.
3. Brown meat and bacon in a small amount of oil, using only small amounts of meat at a time so that the meat

browns quickly and does not stew. Turn so all sides become browned. When all the meat is browned, cut up the large onion and brown it. Add the peeled small onions and brown them.

4. Pour one ladle of marinade into pan to deglaze.

5. Combine browned meat with the onions and rest of the marinade. The marinade should just cover the meat. Add more wine if necessary.

6. Cook in slow cooker for 2 hours at simmer. When tender, work the butter into the cornstarch and then add a small ladle of the sauce to the beurre manié. Add this to the pot and simmer 5 minutes to slightly thicken.

Serving Suggestion: Serve with toasted baguette slices.
Wine: Enjoy this dish with Spicewood Vineyards Merlot Nouveau, Estate, Texas Hill Country, 2002 or later vintages.

25

Ste. Genevieve Wines
Fort Stockton, Texas

If you go . . .
Ste. Genevieve Wines
P.O. Box 697
Fort Stockton, TX 79735
Hours:
Tours and tastings are held
Wednesdays and Saturdays, and must
be scheduled through the Fort
Stockton Chamber of Commerce:
(800) 336-2166 or (432) 336-8525.

Selected Wines
Chardonnay
Sauvignon Blanc
White Zinfandel
Texas White
Cabernet Sauvignon
Gamay
Merlot
Pinot Noir
Gamay
Red Zinfandel
Texas Red
Texas Blush
Peregrine Hill label:
Chardonnay
Cabernet Sauvignon
Pinot Noir
Syrah
Merlot

When driving down Interstate 10 in West Texas, you can't help noticing the expanse of Texas sky, row after row of windmills, and a large rectangular building surrounded by acres of vineyards. Located on the edge of the interstate, one thousand acres of vineyards send a message to travelers that Ste. Genevieve is a serious winemaking enterprise.

It all began in 1983 when the University of Texas leased West Texas land to the Cordier Corporation. The first wines were bottled in 1987. Today, Domaine Cordier, U.S.A. and Cordier Estates, Inc. operate Ste. Genevieve on acreage leased by the university.

The area was selected because of its warm and dry climate and cool West Texas evenings. The warmth encourages production of sugar in the grapes, while the cool evenings slow the rate of maturation. The soil is relatively deep, and the sloping hillsides aid drainage. Grapes are harvested, two varieties at a time, over about a two-month period extending from mid-July until mid-September.

Ste. Genevieve is by far the largest winery in Texas. Wines are bottled in two sizes—750 ml and 1.5 liter. Chardonnay is its most popular white wine, while Texas Red and Merlot rank as the winery's most popular red wines.

Despite the winery's massive size and levels of production, the Ste. Genevieve staff takes great care in the production of its wines, from grape growing through bottling. Winemaker Bénédicte Rhyne closely monitors the wines during each stage of production. Samples are tasted throughout fermentation, and scientific analyses are done in the winery's well-equipped chemistry lab. Tests are also run during bottling to ensure that the wines meet the company's stringent quality standards.

In 2003, the winery launched a line of premium wines under the Peregrine Hill label. Peregrine Hill wines include Chardonnay, Merlot, Cabernet Sauvignon, Pinot Noir, and Syrah.

Ste. Genevieve participates in a number of statewide wine events, as well as local Fort Stockton celebrations. Tours are operated on Wednesdays and Saturdays through the Fort Stockton Chamber of Commerce.

The following two recipes, one provided by Ste. Genevieve and the other provided courtesy of the Texas Beef Council and Ste. Genevieve, offer exciting ways to use Ste. Genevieve wines in the kitchen. The Sangria is a popular party beverage, while the Cabernet Beef has a distinct black-cherry marinade.

 ### Ste. Genevieve Sangria

Makes about ³/₄ gallon

For a white-wine sangria, substitute a Ste. Genevieve white wine and apple juice for the first two ingredients. This recipe is provided courtesy of Ste. Genevieve Wines.

2 cups Ste. Genevieve red wine
One 12-ounce can cranberry juice concentrate
One 6-ounce can orange juice concentrate
Juice of 1 lemon
2 cups water
1 orange, thinly sliced
1 lemon, thinly sliced
1 apple, cut into wedges
1 quart sparkling water

1. In a large pitcher, combine red wine, cranberry juice concentrate, orange juice concentrate, lemon juice, and water. Stir. Add fruit. Stir in sparkling water just before serving.
2. Serve in a glass over ice. Garnish with an orange slice.

 ## Cabernet Beef Jubilee

Serves 4

This recipe is provided courtesy of the Texas Beef Council and Ste. Genevieve Wines. The delightful Cabernet grilled beef is paired with a black-cherry marinade.

1 cup balsamic vinegar
1 cup Ste. Genevieve Cabernet Sauvignon
$^{1}/_{2}$ cup sugar
$^{1}/_{2}$ teaspoon mustard seed
2 strips lemon zest
2 sticks cinnamon
1 cup dark sweet cherries (fresh, frozen, or canned)
Four 5-ounce top blade steaks

1. Combine all ingredients, except cherries and meat, in a saucepan. Simmer over medium heat 10 minutes.

2. Pour $^3/_4$ cup wine sauce into resealable bag with steaks. Marinate steaks 30 minutes to 2 hours. Place remaining wine sauce in refrigerator while steaks marinate.

3. Strain remaining wine mixture (the portion that was not used to marinate beef). Pour back into saucepan and add cherries. After steaks are done, simmer wine sauce 5 minutes to reheat.

4. Place steaks on grill over medium high coals. Grill 4 minutes per side, turning once. Serve steaks with sauce.

To Thicken Sauce: Dissolve 1 tablespoon cornstarch in 1 tablespoon cold water, then add to sauce while reheating.

Note: Other recommended steak cuts include sirloin, strip, and rib eye. For shoulder steaks, marinate 6–8 hours before grilling.

Wine: Serve with Ste. Genevieve Cabernet Sauvignon.

26

Texas Hills
Vineyard
Johnson City, Texas

If you go . . .
Texas Hills Vineyard
P.O. Box 1480
Johnson City, TX 78636
Phone: (830) 868-2321
Website: www.texashillsvineyard.com
Hours:
Monday–Saturday: 10 a.m.–5 p.m.
Sunday: Noon–5 p.m.

Selected Wines
Chardonnay
Due Bianco (Chardonnay and Pinot
  Grigio blend)
Pinot Grigio
Rosato di Sangiovese
Sangiovese 2001 Kuhlken Vineyard
  (Sangiovese and Cabernet blend)
Primitivo 2001 Akashic Vineyard
Tre Paesano (Cabernet Sauvignon,
  Merlot, Ruby Cabernet blend)
Merlot
Syrah
Cabernet Sauvignon
Rossore (slightly sweet blend of
  Chardonnay, Chenin Blanc, and
  Primitivo)
Moscato (pleasantly sweet)

Gary and Kathy Gilstrap and son Dale Rassett welcome visitors to Texas Hills Vineyard throughout the year. There is always something special going on at the vineyard. Go through the wrought-iron gates featuring a gold Texas star, and you know you are in for a delightful wine country visit.

Constructing a winery that is as good for the environment as it is for the wines was important to the Gilstraps. The winery building is made from earth available on the property, called "rammed earth." Only two doors offer a connection to the outside of the windowless structure. Solid two-foot-thick walls make it nearly impossible for heat or cold to flow in or out of this aboveground cave. The tasting room features eighteen-inch-thick walls, and is known for its quiet and friendly atmosphere.

Texas Hills is situated along gently rolling hills reminiscent of the Tuscan countryside, so it is no wonder that the wines have an Italian influence. Varieties of grapes grown at the vineyard include Pinot Grigio, Moscato, Sangiovese, Chardonnay, Cabernet Sauvignon, and Merlot.

Dale's specialty is working in the field, Gary is the winemaker, and Kathy runs the tasting room. Consultant Enrique Ferro provides production advice.

Texas Hills maintains an active event schedule at the winery and throughout the state. The winery participates in wine trail events and hosts a number of celebratory evenings at the vineyard, complete with great food, wine, and entertainment.

The vineyard offers gift baskets stuffed with wines, sauces, and other Texas-themed items. A one-of-a-kind gift is a chocolate-wrapped bottle of wine (Texas Hills Moscato or Merlot). Texas Hills Vineyard and Dr. Chocolate confectionery in Austin team up for this delectable combination, which is available during the holiday season and for Valentine's Day. Imagine this: A bottle of wine is coated with food-grade wrap, which is then dipped in dark chocolate, wrapped in a transparent gift wrap, and tied with a beautiful bow. When the lucky recipient unties the bow, the transparent gift wrap gently cascades downward and folds out, offering a "catch area" for the chocolate. A simple tug on the bottle releases the chocolate, sending it tumbling onto the transparent wrap. Nibble on the chocolate and savor the wine. What a perfect way to say, "I love you."

Kathy Gilstrap shares her delicious recipe for Rosemary Pesto, a delightful blend of herbs and flavors.

 ## Rosemary Pesto

Kathy Gilstrap suggests adding any nut—such as pine nuts, pecans, or walnuts—to the pesto for extra richness and flavor. This delicious pesto adds flair to broiled meats and chicken.

1 cup fresh rosemary leaves
8 cloves garlic
$^1/_2$ cup olive oil
1 tablespoon kosher salt
1 teaspoon pepper
Your choice of meat

1. Process rosemary and garlic in food processor until smooth, stopping once to scrape sides. Add oil slowly in a steady stream. Add salt and pepper.
2. Spread pesto evenly over chosen meat (tastes great on pork tenderloin or chicken breast).
3. Place on a rack in a broiler pan. Roast at 350°F for 40 minutes or until meat thermometer inserted into thickest portion registers 160°F (for pork). Let stand 15 minutes before serving.

Wine: Serve with Texas Hills Vineyard Tre Paesano or Merlot.

27

Wichita Falls Vineyards & Winery
Iowa Park, Texas

Nestled between the rustling waters of the Wichita River and Buffalo Creek, Wichita Falls Vineyards produce wines which capture the unique spirit and history of the region—from the Wia Chitoh Indians to today's international mix of culture and lifestyles.

If you go . . .
Wichita Falls Vineyards & Winery
3399 Peterson Road South
Iowa Park, TX 76367
Phone: (940) 855-2093
Hours:
Tours and tastings by appointment.

Selected Wines
Wichita Red (Cabernet, Zinfandel, and Sangiovese blend)
Viognier
Chardonnay
Petite Syrah
Pinot Noir
Port
Muscat Canelli

Alton and Lana Gates appreciate travel, wines, and the wine country scenery. Their fondness for these aspects of life, coupled with their entrepreneurial spirit, led them to pursue a second career as vintners. Alton retired after thirty-four years at TXUEnergy, and Lana is a schoolteacher currently teaching kindergarten. Wichita Falls Vineyards offers a peaceful setting and the chance to pursue something they love.

The winery, named for the region's waterfalls, is situated just six miles from the town of Wichita Falls. One of the state's newest vineyards, Wichita Falls is sandwiched between the Wichita River and Buffalo Creek.

The vineyard spans three acres and includes these grape varieties: Merlot, Cabernet Sauvignon, Sangiovese, and Zinfandel. Additional varieties used in winemaking are purchased through other reputable growers.

Alton and Lana are excited about offering special events at the vineyard, which provides a lovely setting for weddings, receptions, and other celebratory gatherings. A banquet room (Lana also calls it the "party room") is ideal for dinners held at the vineyard.

Lana and Alton share three of their favorite vineyard recipes—a well-seasoned pheasant or Cornish game hen and two delectable desserts.

 ## Alton's White Wine Pheasant or Cornish Game Hens

Serves 4

Alton suggests you and your guest sip the remaining half bottle of wine while preparing a huge, fresh Romaine salad and bread to accompany your entrée.

2 pheasants (or 4 Cornish game hens), seasoned with salt
   and pepper
1 onion, chopped
2 cloves garlic, sliced or minced
2–3 large carrots, sliced diagonally
1 cup chopped celery
2 large potatoes, cut in quarters
Salt and pepper, to taste
$^1/_2$ bottle Chardonnay, Chenin Blanc, or Sauvignon Blanc

1. Preheat oven to 350°F.
2. Spray a large cast-iron ovenproof skillet or deep baking
dish with butter-flavored cooking spray or vegetable spray.
Place salted and peppered pheasants in the skillet. Place
vegetables over and around them.
3. Pour wine over all. Sprinkle salt and pepper (amount is
up to you) over the top. Cover with foil.
4. Bake in preheated oven 45 minutes to 1 hour, until the
pheasants or hens test done and juices run clear when
pricked. Be careful when removing from oven, as juices will
be quite hot.

Wine: Serve with Wichita Falls Chardonnay.

Muscat Canelli Fruit and Cream

Serves 4

Alton and Lana prefer fresh fruit, but thawed frozen or canned may be substituted. You may also use other fruits in season, such as fresh pineapple, blueberries, raspberries, grapes, pears, melon, or kiwi. Adjust the amount of Muscat Canelli to your taste.

1 cup sliced fresh strawberries
2 sliced fresh peaches or nectarines
1 cup chopped honeydew
$1/2$–$3/4$ cup Muscat Canelli
One 8-ounce carton Cool Whip or whipped cream

1. Place prepared fruits in a deep bowl. Pour Muscat Canelli over all. Cover tightly and refrigerate several hours or overnight.
2. Remove fruit and place in dessert dishes. Pour the Muscat from the fruit slowly into the Cool Whip or whipped cream as you stir the cream and mix the wine to a very smooth consistency. The cream can be as thick or thin as you like, depending on the amount of Muscat you have from the fruit.
3. Place the cream over the fruit and serve immediately.

Wine: Serve with Wichita Falls Muscat Canelli.

Poached Pears in Port Sauce

Serves 4

Alton and Lana developed this recipe out of their love for fresh pears and Port. The beautiful pink pears make a great side dish at Thanksgiving and Christmas, or any time you want to prepare a quick and easy special dessert.

2 cups Port (any good red Port)
4 large pears, peeled, halved lengthwise
1 cup semisweet chocolate chips
One 8-ounce carton Cool Whip or whipped cream
$1/4$ cup sliced almonds, for garnish

1. Bring Port to a boil in a medium saucepan. Add pears and lower heat to simmer for 10 minutes. Remove from heat. Allow to cool, then cover and refrigerate at least 4 hours, or even overnight if serving the next day.
2. To serve, place pears flat side down on a plate. Pour remaining Port sauce over the top.
3. Melt chocolate chips in microwave or double boiler. Drizzle over pears and sauce. Top with a dollop of cream and sprinkle sliced almonds over top.

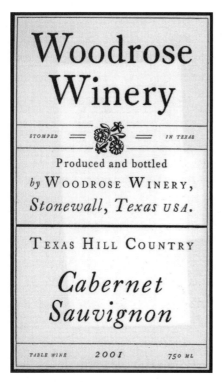

28

Woodrose Winery & Retreat

Stonewall, Texas

If you go . . .
Woodrose Winery & Retreat
662 Woodrose Lane
Stonewall, TX 78671
Phone: (830) 644-2111
Website: www.woodrosewinery.com
Hours:
Thursday–Sunday: Noon–8 p.m.

Selected Wines
Cabernet Sauvignon
Cabernet Rosé

In the beautiful Texas Hill Country just west of the LBJ State and National Park, proprietor Brian Wilgus produces wines using minimal filtration and fining. The "boutique" winery was founded in 1995 and relocated to its current setting in 1999. Its first grapes were planted in 1999, and construction began on the winery and lodge at that time. Grape varieties include Cabernet Sauvignon, Merlot, and Sauvignon Blanc. Woodrose wines have already achieved award-winning status.

The lodge and tasting room, which opened in 2003, are situated among beautiful post oak trees. The design for the winery building was inspired by the LBJ homestead in Johnson City, Texas. The vineyard offers scenic views, large meadows, and spectacular sunsets. Bed-and-breakfast cabins are part of the plans for expansion.

The tasting room is a large lodge-type setting ideal for group gatherings, private parties, weddings, seminars, and vintner dinners. A variety of Woodrose wines, as well as wines from other Texas vintners, are available for purchase in the tasting room and gift shop.

Brian Wilgus shares his recipe for Venison Rouladen, which features Woodrose Cabernet Sauvignon blended with flavorful seasonings.

Venison Rouladen

Serves 6-8

1 large backstrap (loin) or good Venison rump roast
Salt and pepper
3 tablespoons prepared mustard
$^1/_4$ cup onion, finely chopped
6–8 dill pickles, halved or quartered lengthwise
3 tablespoons oil, butter, or margarine
$^1/_4$ pound fresh mushrooms, sliced
$^3/_4$ cup Woodrose Cabernet Sauvignon
1 cup beef broth
2 tablespoons cornstarch
2 tablespoons water

1. Preheat oven to 350°F.
2. Slice roast against the grain, about $^1/_4$ inch thick. Pound with meat hammer to about $^1/_8$ inch thick. Season with salt and pepper. Spread with mustard. Sprinkle with onions; add strip of pickle. Roll up meat and fasten with toothpicks.
3. Brown meat rolls in hot fat in skillet. Add mushrooms, wine, and broth. Cover; cook slowly 15 minutes, adding water if necessary.
4. Transfer to ovenproof serving dish; place in preheated oven and roast 1 hour.
5. Mix cornstarch and water and carefully stir into pan. Bake for another 15 minutes as the sauce thickens.

Wine: Serve with Woodrose Cabernet Sauvignon.

29

Recipes from Chefs

The Texas state capital, Austin, is also known as River City (the Colorado River winds through it), the Live Music Capital, Waterloo (once the city's name), Silicon Valley of Texas, Film Capital of the state, and the list goes on. It is also a center of fine cuisine, reflecting flavors from around the world.

Highly regarded Austin chefs share wine-related recipes in this chapter. Reflecting each chef's culinary genius, the recipes are sure to add flair to any kitchen.

The structure of each recipe is in its original format. Some include suggestions for plating and serving. From the capital of Texas to your home kitchen, lone appétit!

Jeff Blank

Chef-Proprietor
Hudson's on the Bend
3509 FM 620 North
Austin, TX 78734
Phone: (512) 266-1369
Website: www.hudsonsonthebend.com

Jeff Blank is the chef-owner of the renowned Hudson's on the Bend restaurant. Prior to Hudson's, he was owner-operator of

The Wineskin Restaurant in Snowmass, Colorado. He has served as celebrity chef for festivals around Texas, including the 1993 Texas Food and Wine Festival and 1995 San Angelo Food and Wine Festival. He received his culinary education at the University of Oklahoma's Hotel and Restaurant School.

Chef Blank is the coauthor of *Cooking Fearlessly,* by Jeff Blank and Jay Moore, with Deborah Harter (Fearless Press, 1999). Beautiful photographs by Laurie Smith show off cooking methods and the finished product, as well as scenes from the Central Texas landscape. Chef Blank's wife, Shanny Lott, provides whimsical chef illustrations throughout this extraordinary hardcover full-color book. These colorful illustrations are also shown on the restaurant's website, where they are available for purchase. The book features a foreword by Dan Rather, a fan and patron of Hudson's on the Bend.

The following recipe was reprinted with permission from *Cooking Fearlessly.* It features an exciting blend of herbs and spices, and is sure to impress any guest at your table.

Smoked Shrimp and Flounder en Papillote— Chef Jeff Blank

Serves 2

    1 bottle Chardonnay
    2 sheets parchment paper, 16 x 12 inches (to make the bag)
    3 tablespoons butter, softened
    2 teaspoons garlic, minced
    2 tablespoons shallots, minced (substitute onion, leeks,
        celery, or jicama as whimsy moves you)
    2 flounder fillets, 5–6 ounces each

6 shrimp (21–25 per pound size)
2 sprigs cilantro
2 sprigs thyme
2 teaspoons lime zest
1 roasted poblano, julienned
$^1/_8$ teaspoon salt
$^1/_8$ teaspoon pepper

1. Preheat oven to 350°F. Put in baking sheet to preheat.
2. Reduce wine in a small saucepan to $^1/_2$ cup.
3. Fold parchment paper in half to cut a heart shape, and make it symmetrical. Repeat with the other sheet.
4. Butter the inside of each sheet thoroughly. Slightly off center on the paper, sprinkle garlic and shallots.
5. Top each parchment heart with flounder, shrimp, herbs, zest, and poblano, divided equally.
6. Splash with reduced wine.
7. Season each with salt and pepper. Top with remaining butter.
8. Starting at the bottom, fold the edges over themselves (kind of like folding a note in high school), sealing the entire paper bag. One trick we sometimes use is to puff with a straw at one end of the bag to make sure it inflates, then hold it closed with a paper clip.
9. Place on preheated baking sheet.
10. Place in preheated oven for 9–10 minutes. Serve immediately.

Serving Suggestion: For a party, each person can bag his or her own fish.
Wine: Serve with your favorite Texas Chardonnay.

De Andra Breeden

Fresh Chef
Austin, Texas
Website: www.freshchef.net
E-mail: freshchef@aol.com

De Andra Breeden is a personal chef who brings her brand of culinary creativity directly into the homes of clients, including celebrities such as Jerry Jeff Walker and his wife Susan.

Chef Breeden completed an intensive apprenticeship and training program under the direction of international chefs at a five-star resort in Ft. Lauderdale, Florida. After relocating to Austin in 1991, she was a chef at Word of Mouth caterers. In 1993, Chef Breeden was the sous chef, working with Executive Chef Peter O'Brien when the Bitter End Restaurant opened in Austin.

Chef Breeden began her personal chef service in 1994 when she started cooking for Jerry Jeff Walker and his wife Susan, who manages Tried and True Music. She is still cooking for the Walker family, as well as other clients in the Central Texas area. Fresh Chef services include menu planning, related grocery shopping, and in-home meal preparation. Meals are prepared for a range of people, from one individual to enough for a small, intimate cocktail party. Ingredients and menu items are tailored to each client's needs, tastes, and dietary habits. Clients enjoy the convenience of coming home to a gourmet meal cooked right in their own kitchen. Chef De Andra Breeden shares her recipe for Veal Scaloppine with Shitake Mushroom Sauce.

Veal Scaloppine with Shitake Mushroom Sauce— Chef De Andra Breeden

Serves 4

2 pounds browned shitake mushrooms, sliced
$^1/_2$ cup butter
1 bottle Messina Hof Papa Paulo Port
15 fresh basil leaves chiffonade (see Note)
Olive oil
8 pieces veal scaloppine
1 cup flour
1 egg
1 cup bread crumbs
Lemon zest

1. Sauté sliced mushrooms in butter. Add Port.
2. After all Port is added, add basil and let simmer for 45–60 minutes over low heat.
3. Just before sauce is ready, heat olive oil in skillet.
4. Coat veal with flour, dip in egg, and then in the breadcrumbs. Cook veal on each side for 2–3 minutes in a hot skillet.
5. Place veal on a plate and top with the mushroom sauce. Garnish with lemon zest.

Note: Chiffonade refers to a technique whereby vegetables or herbs are stacked on top of one another and cut into strips, julienne fashion.
Wine: Serve with a Texas Merlot or Chevin Blanc.

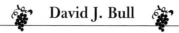

David J. Bull

Executive Chef, Driskill Grill
The Driskill Hotel
604 Brazos Street
Austin, TX 78701
Phone: (512) 474-5911
Website: www.driskillhotel.com

Chef David J. Bull, who received the title "Best New Chef—2003" from *Food & Wine* magazine at age 28, assures that every plate meets his criteria of great cuisine—perfectly balancing taste, texture, and contrasting flavors.

Chef Bull's dynamic, innovative cuisine and impeccably prepared traditional meals continue to receive high praise. His cooking is celebrated by celebrities including Oprah Winfrey, Steven Spielberg, Tom Hanks, and former President and First Lady Clinton. Chef Bull blends a passion for culinary arts and creativity with the freshest, finest ingredients at Austin's Driskill Hotel, which was recently restored to its period splendor.

Chef Bull's appreciation for fine cuisine began when he, along with other family members, worked at Olivieri's, his grandfather's restaurant in upstate New York. There he first learned how to turn out delicious salads and garlic bread. Since then, every job he has held has been in a restaurant. He received his professional training at the Culinary Institute of America, and held positions in a number of prestigious kitchens before joining the Driskill.

Chef Bull worked at the Peabody Hotel in Orlando, Florida, before taking a job at the esteemed Mansion on Turtle

Creek in Dallas, Texas. During his five years at the Mansion, he soared through the ranks to become the youngest executive sous chef in the hotel's history. Working with Chef Dean Fearing, Bull absorbed himself in the "five-star experience," which prepared him for the position at the Driskill.

Chef Bull balances his passion for cultural diversity with classical techniques to bring diners at The Grill an adventure on every plate. "I love to mesh classic techniques and ideas with common, more familiar ingredients, then add extra flavor to create something the average person is comfortable with, but is the absolute best they have ever had," explains Bull.

He has built a top-rated culinary team at the Driskill, where he teaches his staff "to cook from the heart, mind, and taste buds." Chef Bull personally interacts with diners at each table. "I love seeing people enjoy food," he says. "They recognize all the hard work that is put into it. If the food makes them happy, then we've done our job."

In addition to his work, Chef Bull is active in numerous community organizations. He shares his recipe for Jumbo Lump Crab Cake with Poblano-Jicama Slaw and Smoked Tomato Butter.

Jumbo Lump Crab Cake with Poblano-Jicama Slaw and Smoked Tomato Butter—Chef David J. Bull

Serves 4

This dish offers a unique twist on a breaded crab cake. Made with a shrimp mousse and no bread crumbs, the crab cake's texture is key. Instead of being fried, it is baked to offer a very light and fluffy result. After baking, it is placed into a pool of lightly smoked tomato batter and garnished with a roasted poblano-jicama coleslaw. The sweet flavor of the crab contrasts perfectly with the rich smokiness of the butter sauce. The slight spice from the poblano peppers offers a secondary element of flavor to finish the dish.

4 Crab Cakes, 3 ounces each (recipe follows)
8 ounces Smoked Tomato Butter (recipe follows)
1 cup Poblano-Jicama Slaw (recipe follows)
6 ounces Cilantro Dressing (recipe follows)
4 cilantro sprigs

For the Assembly:

1. In four large, warm dinner plates, ladle 2 ounces of the smoked tomato butter into the center of each bowl.
2. Place one crab cake in the center of the butter sauce, and place $^1/_4$ of the slaw on top of the crab cake.
3. Garnish with dots of the reserved dressing and a sprig of cilantro.

For the Crab Cakes:

$^1/_4$ pound jumbo lump crabmeat
1 bunch green onions, finely chopped
6 each U-12 shrimp (peeled, deveined, tail removed)
1 whole egg
1 teaspoon Dijon mustard
$^1/_4$ teaspoon cayenne pepper
$^1/_4$ teaspoon Worcestershire sauce
1 garlic clove

³/₄ cup heavy cream
Salt to taste

1. In this preparation, it is important to keep all ingredients cold until the final cooking stage. Pick through crabmeat to ensure there are no shells, and place in the refrigerator.
2. In a sauté pan over medium heat, quickly cook the green onions; place on a paper towel in the refrigerator to cool.
3. In a food processor, combine the remaining ingredients except for the heavy cream. Quickly pulse until well blended.
4. While running the food processor on high, slowly pour in the heavy cream. It is important that this is done slowly, because the mixture may break.
5. Once the cream is fully incorporated, remove the mixture to a clean mixing bowl. Fold in the crab and green onions.
6. Preheat oven to 400°F.
7. Cook a small dollop of the mixture in a sauté pan, searing it on both sides and finishing it in the oven.
8. Cook until firm to the touch. Allow to cool, and taste for seasoning. Adjust salt content as needed.
9. Using an ice-cream scoop, scoop the mixture into a sauté pan over medium heat. Allow to brown and flip using a spatula; gently press down and allow to brown.
10. Remove and finish in the oven until firm to the touch.

For the Smoked Tomato Butter:

2 Roma tomatoes, rough chopped, lightly smoked
1 poblano chile, peeled and seeded
2 shallots, rough chopped
1 ounce Alamosa Wine Cellars Viognier wine
2 ounces tomato juice
1 bunch cilantro, stems removed
1 ounce heavy cream
$^{1}/_{2}$ pound unsalted butter
Salt to taste

1. Rough chop and purée the Roma tomatoes; place in a medium saucepan with the shallots, poblano, white wine, and tomato juice.
2. Reduce this mixture until almost dry; add the cream and reduce by half.
3. Add cilantro, whisk in the whole butter, and season with salt.
4. Strain the smoked tomato butter through a fine sieve and keep warm.

For the Poblano-Jicama Coleslaw:

2 poblano chiles, roasted, peeled, and julienned
1 jicama, peeled and julienned
1 red cabbage, outside leaves only, julienned
4 ounces Cilantro Dressing (recipe follows)
2 limes, juiced
Salt to taste

1. Mix the poblanos, jicama, and cabbage together; add the cilantro dressing and incorporate.

2. Season with lime juice and salt to taste.

For the Cilantro Dressing:

2 bunches cilantro, blanched and shocked in ice water
12 spinach leaves, blanched and shocked in ice water
2 tablespoons mayonnaise
3 limes, juiced
Salt to taste

1. Place all ingredients into a blender and purée until smooth.

2. Season with salt to taste.

Wine: Serve with Alamosa Wine Cellars Viognier.

Shawn Cirkiel

Chef, Cirkiel Catering, Inc.
(formerly Jean Luc's Bistro, Austin, Texas)

Chef Cirkiel graduated with honors from the Culinary Institute of America and earned experience at such well-respected establishments as Domaine Chandon in California's Napa Valley, Café Boulud in New York, and La Marquesa in Scottsdale, Arizona. Under Chef Cirkiel's direction, Jean Luc's Bistro received outstanding reviews from local and national media including *Bon Appétit* magazine.

Chef Cirkiel uses fresh ingredients, representing cultures from around the world. Known for innovation, he shares his recipe for Braised Pork Shoulder with Roasted Apples, Celery Root, Baby Turnips, Baby Carrots, and Potato Purée.

 Braised Pork Shoulder with Roasted Apples, Celery Root, Baby Turnips, Baby Carrots, and Potato Purée— Chef Shawn Cirkiel

Serves 8

For Braised Pork:

1 pork shoulder, split and tied
Salt and pepper, to taste
1 cup peeled and diced carrots
1 cup peeled and diced celery
2 cups diced yellow onion
1 diced Granny Smith apple
4 sprigs thyme
2 cloves garlic
2 tablespoons tomato paste
$^1/_2$ bottle Becker Vineyards Cabernet Sauvignon
4 cups chicken broth or beef broth
2 tablespoons butter

1. Preheat oven to 350°F. Season pork with salt and pepper. Sear in hot pan until golden on all sides.
2. Remove from pan and add vegetables and apple. Cook on low heat until golden brown.
3. Add tomato paste and aromatics.

4. Deglaze with wine. Add pork back into pan. Add broth.

5. Place in preheated oven, adding more broth if necessary to keep half full.

6. When pork is tender, remove from oven and strain poaching liquid into small pan.

7. Remove fat from liquid and reduce. Add butter when ready to serve.

For Vegetables:

1 bunch peeled, blanched baby carrots
1 bunch peeled, blanched baby turnips
1 cup diced celery root
$1/4$ pound bacon lardons, crisped
3 apples, cut into eighths
$1/4$ cup water
2 tablespoons butter
1 tablespoon chopped parsley
Salt, to taste

1. Place celery root and apples in pan with 1 tablespoon butter. Roast slowly until celery root and apples are cooked.

2. Add blanched vegetables.

3. Add bacon lardons.

4. Add $1/4$ cup water, parsley, and butter.

5. Season with salt to taste.

For Potato Purée:

5 potatoes, boiled and drained
1 cup heavy cream
5 tablespoons butter

1. Combine cooked, drained potatoes with cream and butter.
2. Mash this mixture until well mixed, or purée in blender.
3. Season to taste.

To Finish:

1. Place potato purée in bowl and top with vegetables.
2. Place 1 slice of pork on top, and spoon reserved sauce around plate.

Wine: Serve with Becker Vineyards Cabernet Sauvignon.

 Terry Conlan

Executive Chef
Lake Austin Spa Resort
1705 S. Quinlan Park Road
Austin, TX 78732
Phone: (512) 372-7300
Website: www.lakeaustin.com

Chef Conlan has over thirty years of experience at premier Austin restaurants, and has been the executive chef at Lake

Austin Spa Resort since 1992. His philosophy is to produce enjoyable meals that are healthy and low fat, and can be savored as part of a robust lifestyle.

Fresh vegetables and herbs grown at Lake Austin Spa Resort enhance the textures and flavors of the meals prepared under Chef Conlan's supervision. The menu incorporates a wide range of regional and seasonal ingredients, and provides ample choices for guests.

"Wonderfully nutritious and delicious food abounds all over the planet. Ironically, some of the more technologically advanced countries, with emphasis on fast and convenient foods, have gotten away from many of these traditions, so a big part of our mission is to simply reawaken peoples' interest in the possibilities of genuinely good eating," says Chef Conlan. "I am not interested in diets or gimmicky foods; I want to produce healthy, relatively low-fat, absolutely delicious meals that everyone will enjoy eating on a long-term basis. Not just the best spa food that they have ever eaten, but some of the best food that they've ever eaten anywhere."

Chef Conlan's expertise is shared beyond the resort guests' meals; he also offers cooking demonstrations and tastings in the spa's demo kitchen. He teaches cooking classes throughout Texas as well as a more intensive summer cooking workshop series.

Chef Conlan's articles and recipes appear in a variety of publications, including *Cooking Light, Eating Well, Shape,* and *Prevention.* He has received a five-star review from *Weight Watchers* magazine. Perhaps you have seen Chef Conlan on television (The Learning Channel's *Laurie's Light and Easy,* or the Food Network's *The Best Of* series). He has provided many interviews for regional Texas radio and television programs.

Chef Conlan's newest hardcover book is titled *FRESH: Healthy Cooking and Living from Lake Austin Spa Resort* (Lake Austin Spa Resort, 2002). It is available around the country in retail stores and bookstores, and it is also sold at the resort and on its website. Prior to publication of his newest book, Chef Conlan wrote *Lean Star Cuisine* as well as the 1998, 2000, and 2002 *Summer Cooking Series* recipe books.

Chef Conlan shares a recipe for Coq au Vin. In true spa fashion, he provides nutritional values for this flavorful entrée.

 ## Coq au Vin Sauté—Chef Terry Conlan

Serves 4

This recipe, featured in *FRESH: Healthy Cooking and Living from Lake Austin Spa Resort* by Chef Terry Conlan (Lake Austin Spa Resort, 2003), is reprinted with permission.

In spite of the fact that it takes less than 30 minutes to cook—one-fourth of the time required for its labor-intensive, oven-bound French ancestor—this saucy stovetop supper retains most of the rustic charm and flavor of the original. Using a lean, all-natural bacon without chemicals provides a richness and depth of flavor with considerably less fat than you might expect (2¹/₂ grams of fat per slice). The cast-iron skillet, which creates all the caramelized bits of pork, chicken, and vegetables, helps give added dimension to this home-style bistro favorite.

2 strips all-natural and nitrate-free bacon
2 teaspoons olive oil
4 (4-ounce) boneless skinless all-natural chicken breast
    halves

Salt and freshly ground black pepper to taste

$^1/_2$ cup minced shallots

$^1/_2$ cup diced carrot

$^1/_4$ cup diced celery

2 garlic cloves, minced

8 medium mushrooms, quartered

$^1/_2$ teaspoon minced fresh thyme leaves

$^1/_2$ bay leaf

$1^1/_2$ cups Fall Creek Granite Reserve

2 cups chicken stock, or half beef and half chicken stock

2 tablespoons tomato purée

2 tablespoons flour, dissolved in stock

$^1/_2$ cup drained bottled pearl onions

1 tablespoon chopped fresh parsley

Salt and freshly ground pepper, to taste

1. Slowly sauté the bacon in a cast-iron skillet over medium-low heat until tender-crisp. Remove the bacon and blot dry with paper towels; crumble and set aside.

2. Discard the bacon grease. Return the skillet to the heat and add 1 teaspoon of the olive oil.

3. Season the chicken with salt and pepper and sauté until browned on all sides. Remove from the skillet and set aside.

4. Heat the remaining olive oil in the skillet. Add the shallots, carrot, and celery; sauté until the vegetables are soft.

5. Add the garlic and mushrooms; mix well.

6. Add the thyme, bay leaf, wine, stock, tomato purée, and flour mixture. Increase the heat slightly; cook, stirring frequently, until the mixture thickens and is reduced to sauce consistency.

7. Taste and correct the seasonings. Add the chicken,

bacon, pearl onions, and parsley. Cook until the chicken is cooked through.

Nutrients per Serving: Cal 298; Prot 27 g; Carbo 17 g; 22% Cal from Fat; Sod 520 mg
Wine: Serve with Fall Creek Granite Reserve.

Sam Dickey

Chef-Owner
The Granite Café
2905 San Gabriel
Austin, TX 78705
Phone: (512) 472-6483
Website: www.thegranitecafe.com

The son of a National Rodeo champion, Chef Sam Dickey is well versed on authentic Texas cuisine. His mentors on the "New Texas cuisine" movement include Bruce Auden and Robert Del Grande. These days, Chef Dickey runs the show at The Granite Café in Austin. There, this native of the Lone Star State creates innovative Texas cuisine.

Chef Dickey's culinary creativity was inspired in early childhood, when he spent time in Paraguay, Bangladesh, and other exotic locations. In addition to his rodeo status, Chef Dickey's father served as a USAID officer, while his mother was a spirited home chef and cookbook collector (she has over 3,000 volumes). She inspired a passion for food in her son.

"One of the perks of living in the places we did was that we were able to employ native cooks," Dickey says. "My mother always encouraged them to cook for us like they would for their own families, so I got early exposure to a wild variety of tastes, textures, and traditions."

Sam finds the kitchen a comforting place to observe, learn, and create. He appreciates fresh ingredients, a passion that stems from his days of browsing open-air markets with his mother and brother, Garreth, who is also a professional chef.

At age 18, Chef Dickey was immersed into an environment of "high Texas cuisine" when he cooked under the direction of Executive Chef and James Beard Award nominee Bruce Auden at Restaurant Biga in San Antonio. (Chef Dickey became the restaurant's head baker.)

When he relocated to Austin, Chef Dickey worked at two highly regarded restaurants—Jeffrey's and The Bitter End—before moving to Houston, where he trained under the renowned Chef Robert Del Grande at Café Annie. During that time, the young chef commuted to Dallas on his days off and worked alongside his brother—without pay—at Star Canyon to gain experience under Chef Stephen Pyles. The experience prepared him for his next position at the helm of Ouisie's Table, owned by Elouise Cooper in Houston. It was there he met his wife, Molly, who was the restaurant's general manager. Shortly after they married, the couple moved to Austin and opened Tap Root Bakery, serving such distinguished establishments as Jeffery's and Zoot. Chef Dickey continues to provide bread for over twenty restaurants while running Granite Café.

At the Granite Café, Chef Dickey's goal is to bring unexpected flourishes to Texas cuisine. He shares his Seared Tuna recipe, which transforms the fish so that it "talks Texan," cleverly anchoring it atop fried green tomatoes buoyed by a home-roasted black bean pasilla chile sauce. He uses the Texas landscape as inspiration for creating dishes that burst with innovative flavor combinations, presented with flair.

Seared Tuna on Fried Green Tomatoes—
 ## Chef Sam Dickey

Serves 10-12

Step One—Marinate the Tomatoes:

> Twenty ¼-inch-thick green tomato slices (about 5
>   tomatoes)
> ¼ cup sherry vinegar
> 2 teaspoons salt
> 2 teaspoons pepper

Toss ingredients and let marinate 6–12 hours before
serving.

Step Two—Make Black Bean–Pasilla Sauce:

> ½ yellow onion
> 4 cloves garlic
> 2 teaspoons ginger
> 1 tablespoon balsamic vinegar
> 2 tablespoons soy sauce
> 4 tablespoons red wine
> 1 tablespoon tamarind
> 2 cups chicken stock
> 4 pasilla chiles, seeded, stemmed, and toasted
> 1 tablespoon coriander
> 1 tablespoon cumino
> 4 cups black beans (your recipe or canned)

1. Sauté onions and garlic until translucent. Deglaze with
vinegar, wine, and soy sauce.

2. Add tamarind, stock, pasillas, coriander, cumino, ginger, and half the black beans. Simmer for 10 minutes and blend until smooth.

3. Add the rest of the beans and simmer until nape (sauce consistency).

4. Season with salt and pepper.

Step Three—Make Avocado-Tomatillo Salsa:

6 tomatillos
1 jalapeño pepper
1 ounce yellow onion
1 bunch cilantro leaves
2 cups diced avocado tossed with 2 tablespoons lime juice

1. In blender, process tomatillos, jalapeño, onion, and cilantro to bright green color.

2. Fold tomatillo sauce into the diced avocado.

3. Season with salt and pepper to taste.

Step Four—Crust and Cook the Tuna:

6 tablespoons coriander, toasted and ground
6 tablespoons cascabel chile, toasted and ground
2 tablespoons kosher salt
10–12 tuna steaks (6 ounces each)

1. Combine spices and salt; crust tuna on two sides.

2. Sear in a hot sauté pan to medium rare.

Step Five—Fry the Tomatoes:

    2 cups all-purpose flour
    1 cup masa de harina
    2 cups buttermilk
    2 eggs
    2 teaspoons salt
    2 teaspoons pepper
    Marinated tomatoes (from Step One)

    1. Mix one cup of the flour with the masa, salt, and pepper.
    2. Blend eggs and buttermilk.
    3. Dust tomatoes with flour; drop them into the buttermilk
    and then into the masa.
    4. Fry at 350°F until brown.

Step Six—Plate the Entrée:

In this final step, the entrée is carefully plated in the order
specified. Each plate is garnished with a small amount of pico
de gallo.

    1. Place 2 ounces Black Bean–Pasilla Sauce in center of
    plate.
    2. Place two tomatoes on sauce.
    3. Top with sliced tuna.
    4. Finish with Avocado-Tomatillo Salsa and pico.

Wine: Serve with Alamosa Wine Cellars Viognier.

 Jane King

Foodie
Central Market
North Austin Location
4001 N. Lamar
Austin, TX 78756
Phone: (512) 206-1000

Jane King holds the distinction of being a Central Market Foodie. She has worked with the highly regarded Texas icon of food stores for nearly a decade.

Jane's culinary expertise derives from a combination of living in various corners of the planet and having a passion for great cuisine. She describes a foodie as "an answer person." If customers have a food question, she will provide them with the answer. She also teaches cooking classes at Central Market. In February 2002, Jane and I teamed up to teach a course at the store on Texas Cooking. I discussed the history of various food products, while Jane prepared the food items using Texas-made ingredients and recipes that she developed.

Jane frequently cooks at home, and prefers intimate dinner parties for four to six guests. She likes cooking for her guests, and finds satisfaction when they enjoy her creations. She says, "Appreciating good food and sharing it with others is the best thing in the world."

Jane shares her recipe for Fig and Blue Cheese Salad with Port Wine Dressing, a delightful combination of flavors and textures.

Fig and Blue Cheese Salad with Port Wine
 Dressing—Jane King, Central Market Foodie

Serves 6

3/4 cup Messina Hof Papa Paulo Port
1/4 cup dry red wine
1/4 cup grape-seed oil
3 tablespoons balsamic vinegar
2 tablespoons walnut oil
1 tablespoon red wine vinegar
1/2 pound dried black Mission figs, stemmed and cut in half
   lengthwise
10 (loose) cups mixed field greens
4 ounces Stilton or Maytag blue cheese, crumbled
2 portabello mushroom caps, thinly sliced
1/2 small yellow onion, finely diced
Salt and freshly ground black pepper, to taste

1. Whisk first six ingredients in bowl to blend. (Can be done ahead; cover and refrigerate.)
2. Sauté mushrooms and onions in a little grape-seed oil until soft. Set aside.
3. Bring vinaigrette and figs to simmer in heavy nonstick skillet over high heat. Simmer until dressing is slightly syrupy, stirring occasionally, about 10 minutes.
4. Cool to room temperature (do not refrigerate). Season to taste with salt and pepper.

When ready to serve, toss greens with the dressing and divide between six plates. Sprinkle mushroom mixture and cheese over greens. Place a few figs over each salad and serve.
Wine: Serve with a Texas Cabernet Sauvignon.

 Roger Mollett

Chef-Owner
Fonds de Cuisine
Austin, Texas
Website: www.fondsdecuisine.com

Chef Roger Mollett credits great food and great culinary influences as two factors that inspire his love of both cooking and teaching. At an early age, he learned about home cooking by observing his mother whip up creations in the family's kitchen, and by helping feed harvest crews at his aunt's Oklahoma farm. During Chef Mollett's teenage years, he found inspiration from television chefs such as Julia Child and Graham Kerr. He gained practical experience at various Wellington, Kansas, restaurants.

In the 1970s and 1980s, Chef Mollett had the opportunity to gain culinary arts knowledge from a number of classically trained chefs at top restaurants and hotels in Kansas, Missouri, and Texas. It was during these years that he began teaching classes at the renowned Marshall Fields department store and offering catering services and operating culinary events for the Belgian Consulate in Houston, Texas.

In 1984 Chef Mollett moved to San Francisco, where he discovered interesting neighborhood markets and ethnic foods. He returned to Texas in 1993, and was hired that year as one of the original partners at the first Central Market in Austin, Texas. During his lengthy affiliation with Central Market Cooking Schools, Chef Mollett instructed over 20,000 students (including the author of this book). He founded the "Good Cooks" series in 1995, which enabled students to learn all aspects of basic culinary technique in a variety of subjects ranging from meat selection and preparation to making fresh puff pastry, pasta, soups, and classic sauces.

Chef Mollett was Central Market's first information specialist, or "Foodie," and he developed the store's first demonstration department. He has made hundreds of media appearances in Austin, Dallas, and Houston. Two segments that he created, "Central Texas Cookbook" and "What's Cooking at Central Market," were featured regularly on KXAN (NBC) television in Austin. Chef Mollett has also been featured on television and radio ads in Austin, San Antonio, and Dallas. He authored a monthly column in an Austin newsmagazine, *The Senior Advocate,* for nearly five years. He has also been featured in publications such as *Southern Living, Better Homes and Gardens,* and *Fast Company.*

In 2003 Chef Mollett's long affiliation with Central Market came to an end, and he created Fonds de Cuisine culinary services. His major focus is continuing his love of teaching; he offers classes in Austin and other Central Texas venues. He also offers private cooking instruction as well as catering for dinner parties, receptions, and other events. Those interested in cuisine from around the world may join him on one of the regional and foreign culinary/historical tours that he leads. And after many years of requests from his students, he is working on a cookbook.

Chef Mollett generously shares three recipes—Salmon Corn Cakes, Scaloppine of Pork Tenderloin, and Wine-Poached Pears—all reflective of his innovative approach to cooking.

Salmon Corn Cakes with Roasted Corn Salsa— Chef Roger Mollett

Serves 4

1 pound fresh salmon fillet, pin bones removed

1 cup Chardonnay, Sauvignon Blanc, or other dry white wine

1½ cups (in all) fresh or frozen corn kernels

½ cup (in all) finely diced sweet onion (1015, Vidalia, or similar)

¼ cup diced roasted red pepper

¼ cup finely diced celery (if possible, use the young tender stalks from the center)

4 tablespoons (in all) chopped fresh basil

¼ cup mayonnaise (or more, as needed)

1 teaspoon Dijon mustard

1 large egg

1 cup soft bread crumbs

½ cup olive oil (in all)

½ cup diced jicama (see Note 1)

2 tablespoons chopped cilantro leaves

2 cups concasse tomatoes (see Note 2)

4 large cloves fresh garlic, finely minced

1 large jalapeño pepper, seeded and minced

Juice and grated zest of 1 lime

Sugar, salt, and freshly ground pepper, to taste

1. Place salmon in a sauté pan, skin side down. Add wine. Bring to a boil over medium heat.
2. Reduce heat to medium low and simmer until cooked through (7–8 minutes per inch of thickness).

3. Remove salmon, cool, and remove skin.

4. Gently flake salmon in a mixing bowl. Add $^3/_4$ cup corn, $^1/_4$ cup onion, roasted red peppers, celery, 2 tablespoons basil, mayonnaise, mustard, egg, and $^1/_2$ cup bread crumbs. Mix well, by hand, until salmon mixture is moist but not overly wet (adding additional crumbs, if necessary).

5. Form into eight equal-sized patties, all of a uniform thickness. Cover with plastic wrap and refrigerate 1 hour or overnight.

6. Heat 2 tablespoons olive oil in a sauté pan over medium heat. Add remaining corn, onions, and jicama. Stir frequently until lightly browned.

7. Add remaining ingredients. Continue stirring for 2–3 minutes, or until most of the liquid has evaporated. Season to taste with sugar, salt, and pepper. Set aside and allow to cool.

8. Clean sauté pan and return to medium heat. Coat bottom of pan with 2–3 tablespoons of olive oil. Gently place four salmon cakes in pan; brown for 1–2 minutes.

9. Gently turn cakes, reduce heat to medium low, and continue cooking until cakes are cooked through, 3–5 minutes depending on thickness of patty. Remove and cover with foil to keep warm.

10. Add more oil, if needed, return pan to medium heat, and repeat with remaining four patties.

Note 1: Jicama is a root vegetable native to Mexico. It has a crisp, slightly sweet flavor and retains its texture when cooked. If fresh jicama is not available, substitute equal amount of diced water chestnuts that have been well drained.

Note 2: Refers to peeled, seeded, and diced tomatoes. 1 large or 2–3 Roma tomatoes will yield approximately 1 cup concasse.

Serving Suggestion: Serve two salmon cakes per person, topped with salsa.

Wine: Serve with your favorite Texas Chardonnay or Sauvignon Blanc.

Scaloppine of Pork Tenderloin with Red Wine, Fig, and Cognac Sauce—Chef Roger Mollett

Serves 4

For Sauce:

1 1/2 cups beef stock, reduced to 1/2 cup
1 cup dry red wine
1/2 teaspoon each of grated orange zest and grated lemon zest
1/2 teaspoon crushed fresh garlic
1/2 teaspoon fresh thyme leaves
1/4 pound dried figs
2 tablespoons cognac or brandy
Salt and freshly ground pepper, to taste

1. To reduce stock, gently boil in a heavy saucepan over medium heat. Pour into a heatproof container and set aside.
2. Add wine and zest to pan. Bring to a boil over medium heat. Reduce heat and simmer for 2 minutes. Add garlic, thyme, and figs. Simmer 10 minutes, or until figs are soft.
3. Place the mixture in a food processor (fitted with steel chopping blade), along with cognac and reduced beef stock. Process until smooth; season to taste with salt and pepper. Keep warm or rewarm over low heat.

For Pork:

1 pound pork tenderloin, membrane removed
Salt and freshly ground pepper
Flour for dredging
2 tablespoons olive oil
Garnish: Lemon zest, sprigs of fresh thyme

1. Cut tenderloin into eight medallions. Place each between two sheets of plastic wrap or waxed paper and gently pound to ¹/₈-inch thickness. Sprinkle lightly with salt and pepper.
2. Heat the olive oil in a large sauté pan over medium heat. Dredge pork slices in flour, and shake off excess. Sauté for approximately 1 minute on each side.
3. Serve immediately, topped with sauce and garnished with zest and thyme sprigs.

Wine: Serve with a Texas Merlot.

Wine-Poached Pears with Crème Fraîche—
Chef Roger Mollett

Serves 4

2 large, firm Bosc or Asian pears
4 cups dry red wine
¹/₂ cup brown sugar
One 3-inch stick cinnamon, broken
6 cloves
4 whole allspice berries
¹/₄ cup crème fraîche or sour cream
Freshly grated nutmeg

1. Peel pears; cut in half lengthwise and scoop out core.
2. Combine wine, sugar, cinnamon, cloves, and allspice in a medium sauté pan. Stir to dissolve sugar.
3. Place pears in wine solution, cut side down. Bring to a boil over medium heat, then lower heat and simmer 8–10 minutes, until pears are tender. Remove pears from pan with a slotted spoon. Strain liquid and return to pan.
4. Return pan to medium heat; allow to cook until slightly thickened.
5. Serve half a pear per person. Drizzle with red wine syrup, top with 1 tablespoon crème fraîche, and dust with freshly grated nutmeg.

Wine: Serve with a Texas Port.

30

Interview with Bénédicte Rhyne
Oenologist, Winemaker, and Wine Consultant

Bénédicte Rhyne is the winemaker for several Texas wineries and a consultant to many others. She also offers wine lab services to numerous wineries in Texas, New York, and Chile. Born and raised in Provence, France, Bénédicte completed her degree in oenology (the study of wine) from the Université de Bourgogne in Dijon, France. Prior to moving to Texas in 2001, Bénédicte worked in the wine industry in Europe, New Zealand, and California, where she spent ten years as assistant winemaker and oenologist for Ravenswood Winery.

In this interview, Bénédicte offers suggestions for learning to appreciate Texas wines, and enjoying them as a complement to popular Texas fare. She explains how even the novice wine connoisseur can enjoy the experience of blending food and wine.

In France, food and wine are very important. What rules do the French follow for pairing foods with wines?

France is still very regional. People eat the foods that are native to their region, and local wines complement the local dishes. Through the centuries they have mastered their ability to do this. I don't know if the food adapted to the wine or vice versa. For example, in the Dordogne region, the richness of the regional dish Foie Gras is balanced with Cahors, a wine made from Malbec, which is also a product of that region. In Provence, the regional specialty Ratatouille is served with a dry Rosé produced in the area. In Burgundy, Boeuf Bourguignon pairs well with Pinot Noir, the primary red wine from that region.

When you are cooking and serving Texas wines, is there anything special you keep in mind in terms of matching the wines with the foods?

I go along with the basic international rules of serving a dry white wine or Champagne with the appetizers. In the summertime, I might offer a dry Rosé for this course. I serve a white or red wine with the main course, depending on the spiciness of the dish. For example, if the menu includes a light chicken or fish, I complement it with a dry white wine. If the meal is spicier, the wines progress from lighter to full-bodied reds. I always serve a sweet wine with dessert.

What varieties of Texas wines pair well with popular Texas fare, such as barbecue or spicy foods?

Hot, spicy foods go well with either sweet light Rosé, such as a blush wine, or you can take the opposite approach and serve them with a tannic wine, such as a Cabernet Sauvignon, Primitivo, or Zinfandel.

If the food is spicy but not hot, I serve a Cabernet Sauvignon, Shiraz, Zinfandel, or Tempranillo (Spanish varietal) along with it.

Barbecue can be served with a dry white wine like Sauvignon Blanc, Semillon, or Chardonnay, or a red wine such as Pinot Noir, Sangiovese, or Merlot.

When planning a traditional Texas meal—chicken-fried steak and mashed potatoes—what wine would you serve with it?

I would select a tannic wine to cut the richness of the foods. Examples include Cabernet Sauvignon, Zinfandel, or Malbec.

Which white wine is a good starting point for gaining an appreciation of wine? And what red wine would you recommend for the novice?

Muscat is a good place to start. It is a very perfumed, medium-bodied white wine. When dry, Muscat is a mono-dimensional wine, meaning that it is not very complex and will contain only one or two flavor characteristics.

I recommend starting with a lighter-style red wine such as a Merlot or Pinot Noir, which are not too tannic or acidic for the beginner.

When learning about wines, it is important to think about how the wine will complement the food. Rather than tasting the wine on its own, integrate it in with the meal. This will help you move on to the next category of more complex wines.

Tasting wine should be a wonderful experience. When you move past the mono-dimensional wines to the more complex varietals, you will look for a sensation of an explosion of flavors in your mouth.

When going to a restaurant, what are some things a person should look at when studying the wine list?

Experiment with the unknown! It could be a hit or a miss, but what better way to learn? Ask your waiter for his or her suggestions. If you don't like the wine that you are served, tell the waiter, and more than likely he or she will offer to change it for something else. Go and try new things, within your budget of course!

How do the Texas grape-growing conditions differ from those in California and France?

The most determinate factor between California and Texas is climate. California is more temperate because of the ocean. Texas has very critical changes of weather, which makes it more difficult to control the growing and critical maturity of the grape. In many respects, Mother Nature calls the shots in Texas. It is a little more challenging than California. Although the climate is a lot warmer in Texas, the challenges are the same as in France. There will be some good vintages in Texas next to some poor vintages, all based on what the climatic conditions were that year.

If I wanted to prepare an authentic French meal, what should the menu include? What wines should I serve?

Start with hors d'oeuvres, such as tapenade, olives, or toast with cheese on it, served with a dry (Brut) Champagne. Follow this course with a traditional salade de pommes de terre (potato salad). A French-style potato salad includes such ingredients as olives, tomatoes, ham, and possibly anchovies. Complement the salad course with a dry Gewürztraminer wine. Next, the meal progresses to the vegetable course featuring Ratatouille, a Provence specialty, served with a dry Rosé wine. The entrée, from the region of Burgundy, is Boeuf Bourguignon served with Pinot Noir. The cheese (fromage) course follows, and is accompanied by a tannic wine such as Cabernet Sauvignon, Malbec, Syrah, or Zinfandel. Serve a classic French "tartatin" (upside-down apple pie) for dessert, complemented with a sweet Orange Muscat wine.

In France, the heaviest meal of the day is traditionally served at lunchtime. Lighter fare, such as an omelet and a salad, is eaten in the evening. However, if you have guests for dinner in France, it is customary to serve a larger meal in the evening.

What advice can you offer to help Texans appreciate wine with their meals?

Don't look at wine as taboo. It is supposed to be part of a meal, like the bread or salad. In my family, we drink wine at every meal (not a bottle, just a couple of glasses).

Wine will complement any meal. I remember having a 10-year-old Cabernet Sauvignon with pizza when my brother-in-law and sister-in-law came to celebrate their tenth anniversary. Wine helps digestion and improves the heart (especially the wines with tannins). A very good complex wine will satisfy you very quickly. If it feels like the Fourth of July in your mouth, you will only need a few glasses. On the other hand, mono-dimensional wines make you drink more because the palate is not satisfied. Moderation is the key. Look at wine as a complement to a meal, not a way to get drunk.

Experiment with wines and have an open mind. There are basic rules, but the best way to learn more is to experience different wines. If a particular wine doesn't taste good, don't hesitate to set it aside and move on to a different bottle.

Try to discover your best wine experience. Mine was in 1990 when I was in Cahors, France, dining on the regional specialty, Foie Gras, and drinking a Cahors wine, vintage 1985. I'll never forget it.

Bénédicte, you have a fascinating background. We are so fortunate that you found your way to Texas. What experiences have you had before moving to the Lone Star State?

Currently, I wear the boots of the winemaker for two vineyards, Delaney (since October 2001) and Ste. Genevieve (since

February 2003), and I am a wine consultant for three wineries: Spicewood, Brushy Creek, and Wichita Falls. I also provide wine lab services to a number of wineries.

Prior to moving to Texas, I spent ten years at Ravenswood Winery in California. I was hired there in 1991, and placed in charge of making Pickberry Meritage wine because of my background in France. In that capacity, I worked with Cris and Lorna Strotz, owners of Pickberry Vineyards, to produce phenomenal wine. I was fortunate to be a part of a winery that went from producing 50,000 cases to 600,000 cases. Almost exactly ten years from the day I started, my priorities had changed and I left California in 2001 and moved to Texas.

Before arriving in California, I worked in New Zealand, and then England. When I completed my oenology degree in 1987, I was eager to travel to the United States. A trip to California did not result in a job, so I turned my horizons to New Zealand, where I spent six months as a cellar/lab person, learning the ropes of a much less regulated way of making wine. That really opened my eyes and inspired a passion for exploring winemaking. It was very different than in France, where strict regulations often govern winemaking.

Upon my return to Europe, I made contact with a wine importer. I accepted an offer to work as a sales representative for Berkman Wine Cellars, a renowned wine importer specializing in French wines. After two years, I really missed the harvest, production, and all aspects of winemaking. My instincts told me to try again for a position in California. Joel Peterson at Ravenswood received my resume and I was hired. The winery was in a growth phase, and I happened to arrive at just the right time.

31

Wine and Cheese

I recall my first wine and cheese party. It was 1978, and while my husband Mark and I didn't understand how to pair specific wines with specific cheeses, we somehow stumbled onto some great matches. In any case, it was fun to pull out our wedding-gift cheese platters and adorn them with assorted cheeses and a selection of our favorite wines.

These days, we continue to find pleasure in serving wine and cheese together. The vintage 1978 cheese trays still provide the perfect platform for displaying cheese, crackers, and fruit.

Wine and Cheese Pairing Guide

A wonderful resource for pairing cheese and wine is this guide found at www .texaswinetrails.com. Tom Ciesla granted permission to reprint this easy-to-use chart. (And if you are going on a wine tour, be sure to read *Touring Texas Wineries: Scenic Drives along Texas Wine Trails,* by Thomas M. Ciesla, Regina M. Ciesla, and Steven L. Moore, Lone Star Books, 2003.)

Cheese & Wine Pairing

Cheese	Wine
Baby Swiss	Asti Spumante
Bleu	Tawny Port, Madeira, Sherry
Boursin	Gewürztraminer
Brie, Vintage	Champagne, Sweet Sherry
Brie, U.S.	Cabernet
Camembert	Cabernet, Chenin Blanc
Caraway	Gewürztraminer
Cheddar, Mild	Champagne, Chardonnay

Cheddar, Strong	Cabernet, Rioja, Sauvignon Blanc
Cheshire	Riesling
Chevre	Gewürztraminer, Champagne
Colby	Riesling, Champagne
Cream Cheese	White Zinfandel
Danish Blue	Cabernet
Edam	Riesling
Feta	Beaujolais
Goat Cheese	Sancerre, Vouvray
Gouda	Riesling, Champagne
Gruyère	Chardonnay, Sauvignon Blanc
Monterey	Riesling
Muenster	Zinfandel
Provolone	Chardonnay
Roquefort	Tawny Port
Stilton	Port
Swiss	Gewürztraminer

Source: Reprinted with permission from www.texaswinetrails.com, Thomas M. Ciesla.

The Mozzarella Company: A Great Source for Elegant Texas Cheeses

2944 Elm Street
Dallas, TX 75226
Order by phone or online:
Phone: (214) 741-4072
Toll-free: (800) 798-2954
Website: www.mozzco.com

Texas cheese is the ideal complement to a glass of Texas wine. A highly regarded source is the Mozzarella Company, which combines Lone Star flair with authentic European-style cheese-making techniques. The company has a fascinating story.

When Paula Lambert (the Mozzarella Company's founder) spent time in Italy, she fell in love with the region's fresh mozzarella. On her return to Texas, she looked everywhere for the cheese, but it simply wasn't available. Thankfully (for the rest of us), Paula's determination sent her back to Italy, where she learned the art of making fresh mozzarella by hand.

In 1982, Paula returned to the Umbria region in Central Italy and studied the technique for creating handmade fresh mozzarella. When she returned to Dallas, Paula put her newly acquired old-world techniques into practice, and the Mozzarella Company was born.

Paula initially sold her fresh mozzarella to restaurants. Her workday began with a trip to the dairy to pick up fresh milk. From there, she put her knowledge to work, creating fresh mozzarella and other Italian cheeses. As soon as the cheese was ready to use, she hand delivered it to her clients. Word spread; Paula began selling her cheeses directly to the public and soon gained national recognition. Today the company has a retail store in Dallas and a successful mail order–Internet business. The company's cheeses are also available in select gourmet food markets.

In the years since her first cheese-making lesson in Italy, Paula has made additional trips back to learn more. Today, dairy fresh milk is still used to make her award-winning cheeses, and they are all made by hand. She has gained a strong and loyal following, and remains passionate and enthusiastic about her products.

The Mozzarella Company offers fresh mozzarella, known for its mild, slightly acidic flavor, in a choice of flavors and shapes. Select from balls, latte (packed in water), tubes, or bocconcini (bite-sized balls). Perhaps you would like smoked mozzarella, or mozzarella rolls with fillings, or capriella (goat's milk mozzarella). The website offers a complete list.

In addition to the impressive array of fresh mozzarella cheese, the company makes an extensive assortment of cow's milk and goat's milk cheeses, featuring other enticing Italian, Mexican, and Southwestern specialties.

The Mozzarella Company also sells gift baskets, including the "Wine and Cheese Party," which features an assortment of cheeses and a set of charms to adorn your wineglasses. Other items include cheese knives and unique gifts.

Paula has put her extensive knowledge of cheese into a wonderful book. *The Cheese Lover's Cookbook & Guide,* by Paula Lambert (Simon & Schuster, 2000) is a must-have for any serious kitchen. In addition to the wonderful recipes, the book offers information on buying, making, and storing cheese. The book is available on the Mozzarella Company's website, at bookstores, and through online booksellers. Paula Lambert graciously granted permission to reprint the following two recipes from *The Cheese Lover's Cookbook & Guide.*

Spicy Cheddar Cheese Straws

(Reprinted with permission from *The Cheese Lover's Cookbook & Guide,* Simon & Schuster, © 2000 Paula Lambert.)

Makes about 36 straws

These straws burst with flavor, adding flair to any wine and cheese buffet.

8 ounces sharp Cheddar, shredded (2 cups)
4 tablespoons ($\frac{1}{2}$ stick) unsalted butter, softened
1$\frac{1}{2}$ teaspoons grated onion
$\frac{1}{2}$ teaspoon Worcestershire sauce
3 dashes Tabasco sauce
$\frac{1}{4}$ teaspoon dry mustard
$\frac{1}{4}$ teaspoon cayenne pepper
$\frac{1}{2}$ teaspoon salt
1 cup unbleached all-purpose flour
1 ounce Parmigiano-Reggiano, grated ($\frac{1}{4}$ cup)

1. Place the Cheddar, butter, onion, Worcestershire, Tabasco, dry mustard, cayenne, and salt in the work bowl of a food processor fitted with a steel blade. Process until combined and smooth. Add the flour and pulse just until the flour begins to disappear and the dough is in pea-sized balls; be careful not to overmix the dough.
2. Turn the dough out onto a lightly floured surface. Knead it quickly and gently until the dough comes together. Divide the dough into thirds. Wrap each with plastic wrap and refrigerate for at least 1 hour.
3. Preheat the oven to 350°F. Line a baking sheet with parchment paper.
4. Pat or roll each piece of dough into a rectangle about 6 x 4 x $\frac{1}{2}$ inches. With a sharp knife, cut the dough crosswise into $\frac{1}{2}$-inch strips. Pick up each strip of dough, gently twist it like a corkscrew, and set on the parchment-lined baking sheet, placing the strips 1$\frac{1}{2}$ inches apart. Sprinkle the strips with the Parmigiano.
5. Bake for 12 to 15 minutes, or until lightly browned. Let stand for 5 minutes, then transfer the cheese straws with a spatula to a wire rack to cool.

6. Serve, or store in a tightly covered container for up to 5 days.

Quick and Easy Chicken Breasts with Fresh Mozzarella

(Reprinted with permission from *The Cheese Lover's Cookbook & Guide*, Simon & Schuster, © 2000 Paula Lambert)

Serves 4

4 large skinless, boneless chicken breasts (1 $\frac{1}{2}$ pounds total)
Salt and freshly ground black pepper to taste
2 tablespoons unsalted butter
1 clove garlic
$\frac{1}{2}$ cup dry white wine (such as Fall Creek Chenin Blanc or Fall Creek Sauvignon Blanc)
8 ounces fresh mozzarella, cut into 8 slices
4 sprigs fresh tarragon

1. Wash the chicken and pat dry. Season the chicken breasts with salt and pepper. Melt the butter in a large skillet over medium heat. Add the garlic and chicken breasts and sauté for 6 to 10 minutes, or until the chicken is golden brown on both sides and almost cooked through, turning as necessary. Transfer to a plate and keep warm.
2. Add the wine to the pan, scraping to loosen any browned bits on the bottom, and simmer briefly to reduce to half its original volume. Return the chicken to the skillet and cook for 1 minute. Place 2 slices of fresh mozzarella and 1 sprig of tarragon on top of each chicken breast. Cover

the pan, remove it from the heat, and set aside in a warm place for a few minutes to let the mozzarella soften and begin to melt. Sprinkle the chicken with additional salt or pepper as desired. Remove the garlic and discard.

3. To serve, transfer the chicken to heated serving plates and spoon some of the sauce over it. Serve immediately.

Wine: Serve with Fall Creek Chenin Blanc or Fall Creek Sauvignon Blanc.

 ## New York, Texas, Cheesecake Co.: Delicious Source for Cheesecakes and Peanut Brittle

Visit the Bakery:
New York, Texas, Cheesecake Co.
211 N. Palestine
Athens, TX 75751

Order Cheesecakes and Peanut Brittle:
Phone: (903) 677-6706
Toll-free: (877) 698-9222 (877-NYTXCCC)
Website: www.nytxccc.com

If wine and cheese pair well, can wine and cheesecake be served together?

Absolutely! Cheesecake lovers can have their cake and drink wine too. Muscat Canelli, produced by a number of Texas wineries, shares the spotlight quite well with cheesecake. A reputable source for authentic Texas-made home-style cheesecake is the New York, Texas, Cheesecake Co. You won't have to visit this quaint East Texas cheesecake bakery; the company has a thriving Internet and mail order business. In any case, enjoy a wedge of New York, Texas, Cheesecake Co. cheesecake topped off with a glass of Muscat Canelli wine. Read on for a big slice of information on this famous Texas cheesecake maker.

The history of this East Texas bakery is drizzled with good taste and a few interesting twists. It all started with a bed-and-breakfast inn overlooking the hills of New York, Texas. In 1985, the owner—a writer—served the inn's guests cheesecake made from a century-old family recipe.

Eventually the owner sold the company to two women, who lost the company during a Christmastime disaster. Someone left a freezer door open during a holiday season, and the owners lost thousands of dollars worth of products. After this chilling (or rather, thawing) event, the shop flooded; the owners shut it down until it was purchased by a man named Tony Hartman, who moved the company across the street.

During this time, hundreds of miles away in the West Texas town of Odessa, Bud and Nancy Hicks were loyal cheesecake customers. Bud purchased New York, Texas, Cheesecakes as holiday gifts for his dear Aunt Jo, who lived in the countryside south of Weatherford. He would order the cake and call to tell her when to expect it. On the delivery day, Bud would get a call from his aunt letting him know that she was at home waiting for her cake. Often, while they were on the phone, Aunt Jo would see the delivery truck heading down the road, and she'd yell to Bud, "STOP him! STOP him! Oh, there goes my cheesecake!" Then she would run outside and wave down the truck. Aunt Jo was serious about these cheesecakes. One taste and you will understand why.

Bud Hicks was so fond of the cakes that he and Nancy bought the company from Tony Hartman in May 2000. Bud had retired from his Odessa construction business and was attracted to the idea of owning a company that produced a top-quality product. He and Nancy moved east and became the proud new owners of the New York, Texas, Cheesecake Co.

What is the secret behind this delectable dessert? The answer in a nutshell is that each cake is baked from scratch using the first owner's century-old Pennsylvania Dutch recipe. The original copy of the recipe is worn but still around, written on old-fashioned paper with one corner missing.

Brace yourself for the outstanding flavor assortment: Original, Turtle Praline, Chocolate, Key Lime, Black Forest, White Chocolate, White Chocolate Raspberry, Chocolate Amaretto, Blue Ribbon Blueberry, seasonal flavors Pumpkin and Christmas, Amaretto, Lemon, Strawberry, Raspberry, and Very Berry.

New York, Texas, Cheesecake Co. offers delicious "guilt-free" cheesecakes for those on special diets or people with diabetes. These cheesecakes are also available in a variety of flavors.

All cheesecakes are sold in three sizes—two, three, and four pounds—as well as Cheesecake on a Stick and Preemies (mini-muffin size). The two-pound cake serves six to ten, the three-pound serves ten to twenty, and the four-pound serves fifteen to thirty cheesecake lovers. The cakes are frozen and shipped year-round by two-day air in a cold-pack wrap designed to keep them chilled.

New York, Texas, Cheesecake Co. has won numerous awards and honors and has been featured in local and national publications and on television and radio shows. The cake was named the "Best Mail Order Food Product of the Year" by *Bon Appétit* magazine.

New York, Texas, Cheesecake Co. has expanded its product line to include Margaret's Marvelous Peanut Brittle. Using an old West Texas recipe, Margaret makes this delectable treat by hand in small batches. The crunchy, sweet treat comes in a variety of sizes including the Big Tex, a fourteen-inch Texas-shaped peanut brittle; Broken Big Tex, a Texas-shaped box of peanut brittle, Little Tex, a six-inch peanut brittle state of Texas, and Brittle Bags, filled with chunks of this crunchy bite of heaven. The peanut brittle pairs nicely with Port-style wine, which complements the caramel flavor of the candy.

By the way, New York, Texas, was named around 1860 in good humor because it was the opposite of bustling New York City. The community had not much more than a cemetery and a church.

32

Wine and Chocolate

Chocolate-coated raisins enjoy a place in my heart as a child-hood movie-time favorite. The chewy texture and sweetness of the raisin complemented the chocolate's creaminess and rich flavor. Those two flavors seem to be a match made in heaven—or at least in movie theaters—inspiring me to attempt matching chocolate with wine, which are both made from fruit.

I've learned through trial and error that pairing chocolate and wine isn't as simple as coating a raisin was. A mismatch can result in disaster, where chocolate and wine fail in attempts to share the spotlight, instead resembling two singers performing an off-key duet. The chocolate can be overpowering, completely drowning out the wine.

On the other hand, wine and chocolate that are properly paired form a symphony of complementary flavors, textures, and aromas. Factors to consider include the sweetness of the chocolate, and the presence of other ingredients such as fruits and nuts in the dessert.

It is important to remember the dessert rule mentioned in the foreword of this book: Make sure the wine is sweeter than the dessert. If you simply cannot find a wine that pairs well with your chocolate dessert, serve two dessert courses. I doubt anyone will object.

When purchasing fine chocolates, ask the chocolatier what wine he or she recommends serving with them. If you purchase the Texas wine first, ask for store recommendations or check the website of your favorite Texas winery. Try experimenting. Your own taste buds will let you know when you've hit an award-winning duo. Here are suggestions that offer a starting point.

- *Port* Port-style wines are made by Texas wineries throughout the state. These dessert wines contain a higher alcohol content than regular wines, about 18 percent compared to the usual 12–13 percent. Wineries often sell homemade truffles made from a combination of their Port wine and fine chocolate. Dark chocolate is more intense than milk chocolate, and many Texas Port-style wines stand up to the strength of the chocolate.

- *Johannisberg Riesling* A sweet late-harvest Riesling may work with a semisweet chocolate. Of course, the sweetness of the particular vintage is an important factor. Chocolate Pear Tart, featured in chapter 10, pairs well with a Fall Creek Sweet Johannisberg Riesling (called "Sweet Jo").

- *Muscat* The sweet Muscat wines often pair with chocolates that are medium in intensity. During the holiday season, Texas Hills Vineyard pairs their Moscato (described as pleasant sweet) or Merlot with chocolate in the form of a chocolate-coated wine bottle. The details of this scrumptious pairing (an ideal gift for a wine and chocolate aficionado) are described in chapter 26.

- *Cabernet Sauvignon* This Bordeaux wine is known for its ability to pair well with chocolate, by itself and in blends. I have seen Cabernet Sauvignon accompanying desserts that combine fruits and chocolate, such as strawberries dipped in chocolate fondue. Cabernet Sauvignon is included in my recipe for chocolate Cabernet Cupcakes, which appears in chapter 33.

- *Merlot* A mellow red wine, Merlot is known for its ability to pair with chocolate. In fact, chocolate is a flavor often noted in Merlot wine tastings. Texas Hills Vineyard pairs Merlot with chocolate as one variety available in its chocolate-coated wine bottles (see chapter 26).
- *Champagne and Sparkling Wines* A sweet Champagne or sparkling wine (not Brut) often pairs well with a light chocolate dessert, such as a chocolate mousse or soufflé. A bit of the bubbly adds a romantic touch to candies such as Valentine's chocolates.
- *Zinfandel* If the chocolate candy features fruit flavors, chances are a fruity Zinfandel will pair well with it. This wine is known for its ability to complement the intense flavors of dark chocolate.

 Chocolate Leaves

Next time you make a special chocolate dessert, top it with a display of chocolate leaves using this easy recipe. Place a leaf on a scoop of ice cream or a creamy pie for an elegant touch.

8 ounces semisweet chocolate
1 tablespoon vegetable shortening
Camellia or other waxy leaves, rinsed and gently patted dry

1. Melt chocolate and shortening in top of double boiler.
2. Using spoon, generously coat the underside of leaves. Chill or freeze until firm.

3. Gently peel leaves away from chocolate when ready to use.

Wine and Biscotti

A discussion of chocolate is an excellent segue into biscotti-land. Biscotti are twice-baked (*biscotti* means "twice-baked" in Italian) desserts that have a hard, crunchy texture and are available in a wide assortment of flavors. Double baking creates the crisp texture ideal for dunking. Biscotti are often dunked into coffee and may also find themselves gloriously immersed in full-bodied red wines, such as Zinfandel.

Marotti Biscotti: Authentic New York Biscotti Made in Texas

749 Redwing
Lewisville, TX 75067
Phone: (972) 221-7295
Website: www.mbiscotti.com

Who says you have to go to Italy for *real* biscotti? From its base in Lewisville (near Dallas), Marotti Biscotti bakes authentic biscotti suitable for dunking. Owners Jo-Ann Marotti and Glenn Mancini grew up in New York, where they began selling their traditional biscotti in 1985. About six years later, they moved to the Lone Star State.

Glenn explains that real biscotti are labor intensive. To achieve that classically dry texture so well suited for dipping, the process involves baking and re-baking. First the dough is mixed, shaped into a loaf, and then baked. Then it is cooled and cut at just the right time—and that's the tricky part—before re-baking. If the biscotti are cut too soon, the finished product will be too moist; but if you wait too long, it will be too hard, even by biscotti standards.

Marotti Biscotti cookies are rolled and cut by hand just like they were centuries ago. There is no added butter or oil. The biscotti contain only flour, sugar, eggs, chocolate, nuts, seeds, dried fruits, pure flavors, and leavening.

Marotti Biscotti offers both American and Italian biscotti. The American flavors reflect this country's tastes: Maple Walnut, Chocolate Cashew (deep chocolate with milk chocolate bits and tropical cashews), Lemon Almond, and Chocolate Macadamia. Italian versions include Chocolate Almond Chip, Mocha Nut, Quaresimale, Raisin Spice, Mint Chocolate Chip, Anise, Lemon Poppy, and Triple Fruit and Nut.

 Quintessential Chocolates: Wine and Chocolate Confections

Chocolat
338 West Main Street
Fredericksburg, TX 78624
Phone: (830) 990-9382
Toll-free: (800) 842-3382
Website: www.gourmetfoodmall.com (click on "Candy & Chocolate" link)

Quintessential Chocolates brings chocolate and wine together in liquid-filled confections (other spirits and nonalcoholic liquids are also offered). Liquor-filled chocolates, once a delicacy crafted only in Europe, are made today in the quaint Texas town of Fredericksburg.

Years ago, when Quintessential Chocolates founder Lecia Duke was working as an architect in Nashville, she traveled to Europe and sampled her first taste of liquor-filled chocolates. A caterer on the side, Lecia enjoyed experimenting with flavor blends. She added chocolate truffles to her catering menu, and their instant success inspired Lecia to learn the European art of making liquor-filled chocolates.

Under the direction of a Swiss master chocolatier, Lecia learned how to create liquid-filled chocolates using a centuries-old method. Lecia now employs her own variation of the technique to handcraft fine-quality liquid-filled chocolates. The technique results in a confection that offers three layers of pleasure. The center contains the liquid (such as wine) surrounded by a thin sugar crust, which is then coated with fine dark chocolate. Take a bite and enjoy the contrast of textures, the liquid center, the delicate crunch of the sugar crust, and the rich outer chocolate layer. Each piece is created in a three- to five-day process.

Quintessential Chocolates are attractively packaged in boxes containing six or twelve pieces with a variety of alcoholic and nonalcoholic centers. Visitors can watch Quintessential Chocolates take shape at Chocolat, a quaint shop in Fredericksburg. The chocolates are available for purchase at the shop, via mail order, and online at the website listed.

33

Recipes from the Author's Private Collection

My recipe collection began during childhood, when my mother explained how to prepare my favorite dishes. I wrote my first cookbook, a treasure that I still possess, at age 10. For this chapter, I selected my personal favorites that blend well with Texas wines. Many were handed down from my mother, my sister Barbara developed others, and still others were passed along by my friend Maureen Thacker, a fellow home economist. Each is a favorite in my family. I'm pleased to offer this collection from my kitchen to yours to enjoy with a glass of your favorite Texas wine.

 Appetizers

 Cheese Balls

Makes 30 one-inch balls

This easy appetizer appeals to children and adults. The recipe is from my mother, who made them decades ago. Keep a jar of Old English cheese on hand and you will always be ready for an impromptu wine and cheese party.

Ingredients

1 jar Old English Cheese
1 cup flour
1 stick butter, slightly softened

1. Preheat oven to 350°F.
2. Mix ingredients in electric mixer until well blended.
3. Roll into 1-inch balls.
4. Bake in preheated oven 15–20 minutes. Serve warm.

Wine: Serve with a Texas Brut Champagne or Sauvignon Blanc.

 ## Burrito Wontons

Makes 48 wontons

$1/2$ pound ground beef
$1/4$ cup chopped onion
Half of a 15-ounce can refried beans
$1/4$ cup shredded Cheddar
1 tablespoon ketchup
$1^1/2$ teaspoons chili powder
$1/4$ teaspoon ground cumin
4 dozen wonton skins
Vegetable oil for frying
Salsa (use your favorite store-bought or homemade)

1. In skillet, brown ground beef with onion. Cook until meat is browned and onion is tender. Drain off the oil. Stir

refried beans, cheese, ketchup, chili powder, and cumin into meat and onion mixture. Blend well.

2. Place a bowl of water (a finger bowl) next to you for use while wrapping wontons.

3. To wrap wontons, position a wonton skin with one point facing you. Place a spoonful of meat mixture on center of wonton skin. Moisten index finger in water and smooth water around the inside perimeter of the wonton skin. Fold one point over filling, tuck under meat mixture. Turn in the sides and continue rolling. The moisture on the wonton skin seals the edges.

4. Heat the fat in a deep saucepan or deep fryer. Fry a few wontons at a time in hot vegetable oil (about 375°F), 1 minute per side. Remove with slotted spoon.

5. Drain on paper-towel-lined plate. Serve with your favorite salsa.

Wine: Serve with a Texas Zinfandel.

 Mushrooms Maureen

Makes 24

My friend Maureen Thacker makes these mouthwatering mushroom appetizers for New Year's Eve.

24 mushroom caps (1–2 inches each)
24 mushroom stems, chopped
1/2 cup bread crumbs
1/4 cup grated Parmesan
4 tablespoons butter, melted
2 tablespoons chopped Italian parsley
Salt and freshly ground pepper, to taste

1. Place mushroom caps on cookie sheet that has been sprayed with cooking oil spray.

2. Mix mushroom stems, bread crumbs, Parmesan, butter, parsley, salt, and pepper. Spoon mixture into mushroom caps.

3. Broil 4–6 inches from heat until cheese is bubbly, about 4 minutes.

Wine: Serve with a Texas Brut Champagne, Merlot, or Chenin Blanc.

Warm Winter Wine

Makes about 1 gallon

Two 750-ml bottles Claret wine
Two 750-ml bottles Port wine
24 cloves
3 cinnamon sticks
³/₄ cup raisins
¹/₄ cup blanched almonds
1 orange, cut up
2 cups sugar
16 ounces brandy

1. Pour Claret and Port into large pot. Tie cloves and cinnamon in cheesecloth. Add to wine along with raisins, almonds, and orange. Simmer 30 minutes.

2. Remove from heat. Remove spice bag and strain carefully. Add sugar and brandy.

3. Cover; simmer slowly for another 15 minutes. Serve warm in coffee mugs.

Entrées

Mimosa Chicken

Serves 4

I developed this sweet chicken dish out of a love for the Mimosa cocktail, which is a blend of Champagne and orange juice.

1 pound boneless, skinless chicken breasts
$^1/_2$ teaspoon garlic powder
$^1/_4$ teaspoon freshly ground pepper
$^1/_2$ onion, chopped
4 teaspoons Dijon mustard
$^3/_4$ cup orange juice
$^1/_4$ cup Texas Champagne
2 tablespoons butter, cut into bits
$^1/_4$ cup brown sugar, firmly packed

1. Preheat oven to 375°F.
2. Wash chicken breasts. Pat dry. Place in small baking dish. Season with garlic powder and pepper.
3. Spoon mustard onto top of each breast; spread along top surface.
4. Sprinkle onions and bits of butter on breasts.
5. Combine orange juice and Champagne. Pour over chicken. Bake in preheated oven for 30 minutes. Turn

chicken breasts and sprinkle with brown sugar. Bake 15 more minutes, or until golden brown and cooked through.
6. Remove chicken to platter. Keep warm. Carefully pour sauce into pan. Boil on medium heat on top of stove until sauce becomes syrupy, about 15 minutes. Stir occasionally to prevent burning. Pour syrupy sauce onto chicken breasts and serve at once.

Wine: Serve with a Texas Chardonnay or Texas Champagne.

Chicken Parmesan

Serves 8–10

6 whole boneless skinless chicken breasts, split and
    pounded to $1/4$-inch thickness
Two 32-ounce jars your favorite marinara sauce
2 eggs, beaten
1 cup seasoned bread crumbs
1 pound mozzarella cheese, sliced
$1/2$ cup grated Parmesan
3–4 tablespoons olive oil

1. Preheat oven to 350°F.
2. Place bread crumbs and eggs in separate bowls. Dip chicken breasts in eggs and then in bread crumbs.
3. Heat olive oil in sauté pan. Sauté chicken breasts on both sides until golden brown.
4. Spray cooking oil in two 9 x 13 pans. Place a layer of marinara in pan. Top with chicken breasts, and pour more sauce on top and around chicken. Sprinkle generously with

Parmesan. Top with mozzarella. Repeat with second pan. Bake uncovered in preheated oven 30–40 minutes. Can be frozen and reheated.

Wine: Serve with Cabernet Sauvignon or Sangiovese blend.

 Buttery Onion Sirloin

Serves 4

$^1/_2$ cup butter or margarine
$^1/_2$ onion, finely chopped
2 tablespoons Worcestershire sauce
$^1/_2$ teaspoon freshly ground pepper
One large sirloin steak, about $2^1/_2$–3 pounds

1. Mix all ingredients (except sirloin) in a saucepan. Heat over moderate temperature until butter melts. Remove from heat.
2. Score the steak and place on rack in broiler pan.
3. Brush butter mixture on top of meat.
4. Broil 10–12 minutes on each side for rare, 14–16 minutes per side for medium. Constantly brush mixture on the meat as it cooks.

Wine: Serve with a Texas Cabernet Sauvignon or Zinfandel.

Spaghetti

Serves 4

1 pound ground beef
1 large onion, chopped
¼ cup olive oil
One 6-ounce can tomato paste
One 15-ounce can tomatoes, undrained
1 cup fresh sliced mushrooms
1 teaspoon oregano
Salt, pepper, and paprika to taste
1 cup water
12 ounces spaghetti pasta

1. Brown onion in olive oil. Add meat and brown. Drain off fat. Add tomato paste, tomatoes, water, mushrooms, and seasonings.
2. Bring to a boil. Cover and simmer over low heat 1 hour. Stir to prevent burning. If sauce is too thin, partially remove cover.
3. Bring water to a boil in separate pot and cook pasta during last 15 minutes that sauce is cooking. Pasta is done when it is slightly tender, al dente. Do not overcook.

Wine: Serve with Texas Cabernet Sauvignon, Pinot Noir, or Sangiovese.

Pepper Steak España

Serves 4

This family recipe dates back to my teenage years. I recall that one helping was never enough.

3 pounds beef tenderloin, sliced thin
$^1/_4$–$^1/_2$ cup butter or margarine
1 pound fresh mushrooms, sliced
3 green peppers, sliced into strips
3–4 tomatoes, quartered
One 6-ounce can tomato paste
1 teaspoon oregano
Seasonings: Salt, garlic powder, and freshly ground pepper
   to taste
$^1/_4$ cup high-quality Texas Port

1. Brown meat in 2 tablespoons butter. Add seasonings and cook over low to medium heat until meat is tender. Set aside.
2. In separate skillet using 2 tablespoons butter, sauté green pepper, mushrooms, and tomatoes for 5 minutes.
3. Add vegetables to meat skillet. Mix in tomato paste.
4. Heat thoroughly and let simmer until green peppers are cooked, not more than 15 minutes.
5. Add Port, stir, and serve at once over steamed rice.

Wine: Serve with a Texas Cabernet Sauvignon or Zinfandel.

Barbie's Brisket

Serves about 8

People travel miles for the brisket made by my sister, Barbara Gore. This recipe tastes best the second day, so prepare it a day ahead. If you have some left over, try my sister's "Barbie-Q" Sandwiches.

4–6 pound beef brisket, first cut
2 teaspoons Lawry's Seasoned Salt
1 teaspoon garlic powder
1 large onion, sliced
1 green pepper, sliced
2 carrots, cut in chunks
1 celery stalk, cup up
3–4 tablespoons soy sauce
$^1/_4$ cup water

1. Preheat oven to 400°F.
2. Place brisket in baking dish or roasting pan. Add all ingredients. Cook uncovered in preheated oven for 30 minutes. Reduce oven temperature to 350°F and cover.
3. Cook with occasional turning for about $2^1/_2$–3 hours or until brisket is tender (test with fork). Add additional water as needed if the juices dry up.
4. Strain gravy and discard vegetables. Cool meat for several hours or overnight.
5. When cool, slice thinly and heat up gravy separately.
6. Pour some (not all) gravy in pan. Add sliced brisket and heat in oven, covered, at 350°F for about 30 minutes.
7. When serving, pass gravy separately.

Wine: Serve with a Texas Zinfandel or Cabernet Sauvignon.

Barbie-Q Beef Sandwiches

Serves 4 (makes about 2 cups sauce)

    3 tablespoons vegetable oil
    1 onion, medium to large size, sliced
    4 stalks celery, sliced
    3 tablespoons dark brown sugar
    2 tablespoons vinegar
    2 tablespoons Worcestershire sauce
    1 cup water
    1 cup ketchup
    1 pound cooked brisket
    4 French rolls

1. Heat oil in 2 quart saucepan. Sauté celery and onion until slightly soft. Add remaining ingredients, except for meat. Simmer for $1/2$ hour.
2. Strain and discard vegetables. Add sliced beef and heat.
3. Serve on French rolls with plenty of napkins on the side. Mmmmm . . .

Wine: Serve with a Texas Zinfandel or Gewürztraminer.

 ## Texas Slow Cooker Chili

Serves 6

    3 pounds stew meat (chuck) or 3 pounds boneless chuck,
        cut into 1-inch chunks
    1 large onion, chopped (optional)

4 tablespoons chili powder
4 tablespoons flour
1 teaspoon dried oregano
2 teaspoons cumin seeds
2–3 cloves garlic, finely minced
1¹/₂–3 cups beef broth (canned is fine)
Condiments: Serve with grated cheese, chopped onions, sour cream, and lime wedges.

1. Combine chili powder and flour.
2. Place meat into slow cooker. Sprinkle chili and flour mixture over meat. Add remaining ingredients.
3. Cook on low setting for 10–12 hours or until meat is tender and becomes shredded. Check broth level as it cooks, and add more if chili becomes too dry.
This recipe freezes well.

Wine: Serve with a Texas Shiraz or Zinfandel.

 Soups

Easy Potato Parmesan Soup

Serves 1–2

1 can Campbell's Select Creamy Potato Soup
1–2 tablespoons shredded Parmesan
¹/₄ cup croutons

1. Heat soup according to package directions. Do not add water.
2. When heated, stir in Parmesan. Ladle into two cups or one large bowl.
3. Top with croutons.

Wine: Serve with a Texas Johannisberg Riesling or Chardonnay.

 Creamy Corn Soup

Serves 4

Two 14-ounce cans corn, drained
2 cups milk or half-and-half
$^{1}/_{4}$ cup chopped onion
2 tablespoons butter
2 tablespoons flour
Salt and pepper, to taste
One 14$^{1}/_{2}$-ounce can chicken broth
$^{1}/_{2}$ pound grated Monterey Jack cheese (or Pepper Jack)
Dash of Tabasco sauce
$^{1}/_{2}$ cup bacon bits (or 6 slices cooked bacon, cut up)
12 tortilla chips, broken

1. Sauté onion in butter until transparent. Stir in corn. Add flour, salt, and pepper. Cook 1 minute.
2. Gradually add broth and mix well. Slowly stir in milk until thickened. Add Tabasco. Add cheese. Stir over low heat until melted.

3. To serve, ladle into bowls. Top with bacon bits and tortilla chips.

Wine: Serve with White Zinfandel or Chardonnay.

Side Dishes

 Broiled Tomatoes

Serves 4

These delicious tomatoes are an ideal accompaniment to a juicy steak.

2 large tomatoes
1 cup bread crumbs
$^1/_4$ cup butter, melted
Salt and freshly ground pepper, to taste
4 fresh basil leaves, sliced thin
4 slices mozzarella cheese

1. Cut tomatoes in half. Scoop out the seeds and make a small hollow. Set aside.
2. Mix bread crumbs with melted butter. Stir in salt, pepper, and basil. Spoon into each tomato. Top with a slice of cheese.
3. Broil until tomatoes are warm and cheese is melted and golden.

Wine: Serve with a Cabernet Sauvignon, Zinfandel, or Sangiovese.

Rice and Cheese Casser-olé

Serves 12

6 cups cooked Texmati rice
8 ounces Monterey Jack cheese, shredded
8 ounces cheddar cheese, shredded
One 4-ounce can diced chiles
$^1/_2$ teaspoon salt
$^1/_4$ teaspoon pepper
2 cups sour cream

1. Preheat oven to 350°F.
2. Combine cooked rice, cheeses, chiles, salt, and pepper in large bowl. Stir in sour cream. Blend well.
3. Spoon into large greased baking dish. Pack down with back of spoon. Bake in preheated oven 20–30 minutes or until set and heated through.

Wine: Serve with Gewürztraminer.

 ## Green Beans Vinaigrette

Serves 6

1 pound fresh green beans, ends trimmed off
$^1/_4$ cup lemon juice or wine vinegar
$^1/_2$ cup olive oil
Salt and freshly ground pepper, to taste
1 tablespoon minced chives
1 clove garlic, minced finely

1. Boil a pot of salted water. Add beans and cook about 6 minutes, or just until they reach the tender stage. Drain and immediately run under cold water. Pat dry. Place in bowl and set aside.

2. Combine lemon juice, oil, salt, pepper, chives, and garlic. Mix well.

3. Stir marinade into green beans. Refrigerate at least 2 hours, or up to one full day.

4. Serve chilled.

Wine: Serve with a Texas Sauvignon Blanc.

 ## Desserts

Remember the cardinal rule of serving wines with dessert: Make sure the wine is sweeter than the dessert.

 ## Cabernet Cupcakes

Makes 12 cupcakes (24 mini-sized)

6 tablespoons cocoa
2 cups flour
1$\frac{1}{2}$ cups sugar
1 teaspoon baking soda
$\frac{1}{8}$ teaspoon salt
2 eggs, well beaten
$\frac{3}{4}$ cup butter, melted (may substitute margarine)
$\frac{1}{2}$ cup water or milk
$\frac{1}{2}$ cup of your favorite Texas Cabernet Sauvignon
1 teaspoon vanilla

1. Preheat oven to 375°F.
2. Mix first five ingredients into mixing bowl.
3. In a separate bowl, mix melted butter, water (or milk), vanilla, wine, and eggs. Add to flour mixture, but do not stir until all of the ingredients are in the bowl. Then beat well.
4. Pour into lined muffin pan. Bake 20 minutes in preheated oven.
5. Frost with your favorite chocolate or vanilla frosting.

 ## Mom's Special Valentine Cookies

Makes about 30 cookies

For Cookies:

1 cup butter or margarine
2 cups sugar
$^1/_4$ teaspoon salt
$^1/_2$ teaspoon vanilla
1 egg
1 cup sour cream
$4^1/_2$ cups flour
1 teaspoon baking powder
$^1/_2$ teaspoon baking soda
1 bag Valentine's conversation hearts

1. Cream butter and sugar with salt and vanilla. Beat in egg.
2. In separate bowl, mix flour, baking powder, and baking soda.
3. Gradually add flour mixture to butter mixture alternately

with sour cream, starting and ending with the flour, beating well after each addition.

4. When dough is thoroughly mixed, chill it for a few hours.

5. Preheat oven to 375°F.

6. Roll chilled dough to ¼-inch thickness. Cut with 2- or 3-inch heart-shaped cutter.

7. Bake in preheated oven 10–12 minutes. Cool on racks.

8. Ice cookies when completely cool. Place one Valentine conversation heart in the center of each cookie, or decorate as desired.

For Icing:

1 cup powdered sugar, sifted
1½ tablespoons very soft butter
1 teaspoon vanilla
Dash of salt
Milk (enough for desired consistency)

1. Blend sugar (a small amount at a time) into butter. Add a dash of salt.

2. When sugar is thoroughly mixed, blend in vanilla.

3. Add milk to desired consistency.

4. Spread icing on cooled cookies.

Wine: Say "Happy Valentine's Day" with these cookies and a festive Texas Champagne or Muscat Canelli.

Date Bars

Makes 16 bars

$^1/_2$ cup butter, melted
$^3/_4$ cup sugar
1 egg
1$^1/_4$ cups flour
1 teaspoon baking powder
$^1/_2$ teaspoon salt
1 cup (8 ounces) chopped dates
$^1/_2$ cup chopped nuts, optional

1. Preheat oven to 350°F.
2. Grease 8- or 9-inch square baking pan.
3. Mix sugar, melted butter, and egg; add remaining ingredients. Spread into prepared pan.
4. Bake 25–35 minutes, or until toothpick inserted comes out clean.

Wine: Serve with a sweet Texas Johannisberg Riesling.

 ## Sour Cream Chocolate Chip Cookies

Makes 3$^1/_2$ dozen cookies

2 cups sugar
1 cup shortening
2 large eggs
1 cup sour cream
$^1/_2$ teaspoon vanilla

$^1/_2$ teaspoon baking soda
4 teaspoons baking powder
$4^1/_2$ cups flour
$^1/_4$ teaspoon salt
One 12-ounce bag semisweet chocolate chips
$^1/_2$ cup chopped Texas pecans (optional)

1. Preheat oven to 350°F.
2. Cream sugar and shortening. Add eggs one at a time, beating well after each addition. Stir in sour cream and vanilla. Blend well.
3. Sift baking soda, baking powder, flour, and salt. Stir into butter-egg mixture. Blend in chocolate chips.
4. Drop by tablespoons onto greased cookie sheet.
5. Sprinkle with nuts (if using).
6. Bake in preheated oven 20 minutes. Cookies should be large, soft, and fairly thick.

Wine: Serve with a Texas Port-style wine.

 ## Maureen's Chunky Chip Cookies

Makes 18–24 large cookies

This recipe is from my dear friend Maureen Thacker.

1 cup butter, softened
1 pound dark brown sugar
1 teaspoon vanilla
2 large eggs
2^1/$_2$ cups flour
1 teaspoon baking soda
1 teaspoon baking powder
1 teaspoon salt
12-ounce package semisweet chocolate chips
4 ounces dark chocolate, broken into chunks (about ^{1}/$_2$-inch chunks)
1^1/$_2$–2 cups Texas pecans (optional)
Cream (to thin dough, if needed)

1. Preheat oven to 350°F.
2. Cream together butter, brown sugar, and vanilla.
3. Beat eggs and add to sugar mixture.
4. Mix together flour, baking soda, baking powder, and salt. Add gradually to sugar mixture. If mixture is too thick, add a few tablespoons of cream.
5. Stir in chocolate chips. Mix well. Stir in chocolate chunks. Mix well.
6. Add pecans if using.
7. Drop tablespoons of dough onto shiny, ungreased cookie sheets. Bake in preheated oven 10–12 minutes. Cookies will seem underdone. (If oven is slow, try 375°F.)

Wine: Serve with a Texas Port-style wine.

English Toffee Cookies

Makes about 36 squares

For Cookies:

¹/₂ pound butter
1 cup brown sugar, firmly packed
1 egg
1 teaspoon vanilla
2 cups flour

For Topping:

12-ounce bag of chocolate chips
1 cup Texas pecans, chopped

1. Preheat oven to 375°F.
2. Cream butter and sugar until fluffy. Add egg and vanilla.
3. Stir in flour until evenly mixed.
4. Pat dough into 15 x 10 jelly roll pan (a cookie sheet with sides).
5. Bake in preheated oven 25 minutes.
6. Remove from oven and while still hot, spread with the chocolate chips. Sprinkle nuts on top.
7. Cut into squares while still warm.

Wine: Caramel desserts, such as these cookies, pair well with high-quality Texas Port-style wine.

Instant Cookies

Makes about 3 dozen

For Cookies:

> 1 cup butter or margarine
> 1 cup brown sugar
> 1 teaspoon vanilla
> 1 egg
> 2 cups flour

1. Preheat oven to 350°F.
2. Cream butter and sugar. Stir in egg and vanilla. Blend well.
3. Blend in flour. Spread into an ungreased 15 x 10 jelly roll pan (a cookie sheet with sides).
4. Bake in preheated oven 20 minutes.
5. Spread with powdered sugar icing while warm. Cool and cut into bars.

For Icing:

> 1 cup powdered sugar, sifted
> 1½ tablespoons very soft butter
> 1 teaspoon vanilla
> Dash of salt
> Milk (enough for desired consistency)

1. Blend sugar (a small amount at a time) into butter. Add a dash of salt.

2. When sugar is thoroughly mixed, blend in vanilla.

3. Add milk to desired consistency, and spread icing on cooled cookies.

Wine: Serve with a Texas Port-style wine.

Appendix A

Tips on Touring Wineries in Texas

1. There are seven regions (called viticultural areas) where wine is grown in Texas:

- Bell Mountain—the first Texas appellation, 5 square miles located in northeast Gillespie County
- Fredericksburg—110 square miles in the Fredericksburg, Texas, area
- Texas Hill Country—the nation's second largest viticultural area, covering 15,000 square miles
- Escondido Valley—in West Texas, stretching for 50 square miles along Interstate 10 in Pecos County
- Texas High Plains—central and western Texas Panhandle, covering 12,000 square miles
- Davis Mountains—falls to the southwest of the Escondido Valley viticultural area in West Texas
- Mesilla Valley—north and west of El Paso (also includes a chunk of New Mexico)

The viticultural areas in Texas cover too many square miles to enjoy on a weekend jaunt. Choose an area to visit, and research the wineries within that region.

2. Winery hours change. Call ahead to be sure they are open when you want to visit. Also, check the websites for maps to the wineries.

3. Some wineries have tasting fees. Check their websites or call ahead to determine fees.

4. Wines don't travel well, especially in the heat of the Texas summer. Wineries warn that a bottle can "spoil" if left in a hot car for as little as twenty minutes. One of my best purchases was a cooler that plugs into the car's cigarette lighter. No bags of ice are needed, and the wines are held at refrigerator (not freezer) temperatures.

5. Check the special events listed on the wineries' websites. If you like vintner dinners and other wine-related events, plan a trip to coincide with an activity that appeals to you.

6. If the winery has a bed-and-breakfast facility, by all means try to book a room there. Often, the room fee includes a bottle of wine in addition to breakfast (vintners are generally fabulous chefs, so breakfast will most likely be divine). Call ahead to reserve, and ask about the rules regarding children and pets. If the winery does not provide overnight accommodations, ask the folks who work there for recommendations.

7. Bring a sweater. Wine cellars are kept cool (a treat in the Texas heat). If you tend to get cold in air-conditioned conditions, you'll appreciate a sweater during the cellar portion of the winery tour.

8. Start a collection of wineglasses etched with the name of the winery you are visiting. They are generally reasonably priced, and serve as a memento of your visit. Instead of using wineglass charms at your next wine tasting, you can simply give each guest a glass from a different winery. Great icebreaker!

9. State law prohibits the sale of wine before noon on Sunday. For that reason, tasting rooms with Sunday hours don't open their doors until after the clock strikes twelve.

10. Above all, please keep our Texas roads safe. It's a good idea to have a designated driver along for the wine tour.

Appendix B

Wine-Tasting Tips

Wine snobbery went out of fashion with the leisure suits of the seventies. These days, it is perfectly acceptable to admit that wines are complex and that there is a lot to learn (that's why restaurants have sommeliers, to help us select appropriately).

You've seen people make various motions with their wineglasses, tipping them, spinning them around, sticking their noses inside. Without knowing the proper technique, the process may seem intimidating, especially in public. But it isn't difficult, even for the novice. Simply sit back and enjoy the three steps: sight, smell, and taste. My sommelier cousin, Pamela Cohen, offered these tasting tips when I decided to crack the mystique and understand what all those motions mean.

Step 1: Sight

The purpose of using your sight is to check out the clarity and color of the wine. Hold your glass at a forty-five degree angle, preferably over a white background such as a blank sheet of computer paper, or even a pure white napkin. It is important to do this step before sipping because you are looking for impurities, for color gradation, and you want to be sure that nothing travels from the glass into your mouth, except the wine.

Ideally, the wine will be clear, although you may notice

some forms of sediment. White wine may contain crystallized tartrates, which occur when the wine is not cold stabilized. Reds may have pigmentation sediment, which could end up as a deposit at the bottom of the glass. Although these deposits are by no means harmful, they may be seen as an unpleasant addition to your glass of wine.

You should be able to see through most wine. If it is cloudy, ask your sommelier for his or her opinion. If it's a red wine that's opaque, this may just be a feature of a deeply pigmented grape variety. Opaque and clear is fine. Opaque and cloudy may be a sign of a problem.

After checking out the clarity and deposits, study the color. Is the white wine a pale yellow? Or deeper in color? Is the wine at the center of the glass the same shade as the wine around the edge? Younger white wines tend to be paler in color than those that have aged a longer time. The opposite is true in red wines, which are deeper in color in their younger stages, with the rim showing orange or brown as the wine begins to show signs of age (a few grape varieties will produce a naturally orange rim, even in youth). Color may also give you a clue about whether the wine was produced in a warmer region of the world or a cooler region. In general, the warmer the region, the more color is produced by the grape, resulting in more color in the wine.

The next part of the sight step is the infamous "swirl." Holding the glass by its stem, gently swirl the bowl (unless it is a sparkling wine) to check out its legs (streams of wine that travel vertically in the glass). Fatter, clinging legs may indicate that the wine contains higher levels of sugar or alcohol, or both. All great wines have great legs, although all wines with good legs are not necessarily great wines.

Step 2: Smell

In the smell step, the swirl is performed again, this time to allow the wine to release its aroma or bouquet. (I find it fascinating that if you smell a glass of wine, then swirl it and smell again, the difference is remarkable.)

Lower your nose into the bowl and sniff until you have captured the aroma. Wine is fruit that has sometimes been aged in wood (oak). You are trying to pick up the aromas of the fruit, spice, and wood. Strong, flowery aromas, or fresh fruit such as citrus, may indicate younger wines that have been fermented in steel tanks. Younger wines tend to have more prominent fruity aromas, a character that mellows and gains complexity with age. Aromas such as butter, smoke, toast, or cinnamon may indicate that the wine was aged in oak.

It is said that a fine wine should impart characteristics of the fruit and soil in which it has grown. The longer it has aged, the more secondary and tertiary aromas become evident, where the fruity aromas have given way to scents that may include leather, tobacco, vanilla, tar, and earth. (Hint: It is imperative that your nose be clear, free from the effects of virus or allergies.)

Step 3: Taste

Again it's time to swirl, this time in your mouth. Resist the urge to swallow, and let a sip of wine float around your mouth. (In a true tasting, you would spit it out rather than swallow.) As the wine travels around your oral cavity, it sails over your taste buds, bringing forth a variety of sensations. The front of the tongue houses the sweet-sensing taste buds, salty buds are on the sides of the tongue, and bitter buds are at the rear of the tongue. Some features of the wine have different effects on the tongue. Alcohol may make the tongue feel hot, while a tongue that stays wet after the spit indicates that the wine has good acidity. Although wine does not typically have salty characteristics, there are certain white wines that one may perceive as having been made or grown near the sea. It should be no surprise that these wines are a natural match for seafood.

If the wine seems to coat your tongue or feels full in your mouth, it is full bodied. If—*Boom!*—your mouth shuts quickly and feels dry, it has most likely been exposed to tannins in wine, and the wine is probably a young red. Red wines contain the tannins that were originally found in the grape's skins, seeds, and stems. Tannins are also present in barrels, with stronger tannins found in newer barrels. Tannins are a necessary component for developing a red wine's complexity and aging potential. A younger wine has more tannins than one that has had a chance to age. The drying sensation caused by tannins is most readily felt by the gums. Once the acids and tannins have had a chance to age, chemical changes take place that bring the wine into greater balance. The wine tastes "smoother," and the flavors and aromas become more integrated.

Now think about how long the flavor lasts. The "length" of the wine is often an indicator of its quality. The longer the flavor lingers, the greater the chance that you are drinking a wine of better quality.

Congratulations! You have sniffed and swirled your way toward furthering your knowledge of wine. Now it's time to sit back, relax, and enjoy. Cheers!

Appendix C

Cooking with Wine

Cooking with wine incorporates the complex flavors of the wine into the food, resulting in taste sensations that delight the palate. Here are some general guidelines about cooking with wine.

1. If the wine is not good enough to drink, it is not good enough to use as a cooking ingredient. The best meals are derived from the finest ingredients. Be sure the wine in your cooking is suitable for drinking. Cooking will not improve a wine's flavor or characteristics.

2. When a wine is cooked, it tends to become sweeter as the sugars concentrate.

3. The alcohol level in wine is lowered as the wine cooks.

4. Spicy wines can hold up to spicy seasonings.

5. Make sure the seasonings do not drown out the wine.

6. The flavors of wines can change with cooking. To maintain the wine's flavor, try to add it close to the end of the cooking time.

7. Cooking can change the color of a wine. This is especially true for the reds, which can become too dark with overcooking.

8. Cook with sweet wines to balance salty flavors.

Appendix D

Wine and Food Pairing Guidelines

You've heard the rule: White wines with chicken and fish; red wines with red meats. Actually, this is one rule that is meant to be broken. There are some whites that hold up to red meats, and vice versa. Pinot Noir, a light red wine, is known for its ability to pair with fish, such as salmon.

You've probably heard the terms "a Burgundy wine" or "a Bordeaux." Both names refer to regions in France where grapes are grown. The Bordeaux region, with about 250,000 acres, is the largest grape-growing region in the world. A number of Texas wineries use a Bordeaux style of winemaking. The five main grapes that make up Bordeaux red wines are Merlot, Cabernet Sauvignon, Cabernet Franc, Petit Verdot, and Malbec. Two white varieties account for most of the Bordeaux white wines—Sauvignon Blanc and Semillon. In Bordeaux, a wine estate is known as a chateau, while in Burgundy it is known as a domaine. The major red grape of Burgundy is Pinot Noir, and the major white grape is Chardonnay.

Champagnes, or sparkling wines, are produced by the méthode champenoise by several Texas wineries. In order to state on the bottle that the champagne is produced by this method, the vintner must follow strict guidelines, the gist of which is as follows: Champagne undergoes two fermentations; the second one results in those wonderful bubbles. In the méthode champenoise, the wine must have its second fermentation in the bottle in which it is to be sold. When the second fermentation is complete, the bottle must undergo two processes—riddling and dégorgement. Riddling involves gently shaking and rotating the bottle, causing the sediment to lodge in the neck. Dégorgement occurs when the neck is placed in a solution that is quite cold, below freezing. The sediment becomes contained in a block of ice that forms at the neck of the bottle. The bottle is opened, the ice plug and sediment removed, and the cork and wire are installed.

The following list offers general suggestions for pairing wines with foods. Remember that your pairings will be influenced by your personal preferences and the sauces prepared with the meats, chicken, and fish.

 ## White Wines

- *Chardonnay* A popular wine, full-bodied Chardonnay is golden in color, and the texture is crisp. Try it with chowders, tuna steaks, and grilled chicken. It can usually hold up to garlicky dishes. Chardonnay is the main white wine of Burgundy.
- *Sauvignon Blanc* Sauvignon Blanc, a white Bordeaux, is a light- to medium-bodied wine that pairs well with chicken, seafood, pasta, and salads. If aged in oak, it can hold up to richer foods. Sauvignon Blanc is a popular cocktail party wine because it pairs well with a number of appetizers.
- *Chenin Blanc* Chenin Blanc ranges from dry to sweet and pairs well with fish, poultry, and seafood.
- *Gewürztraminer* This spicy German wine can range from

dry to semisweet. It pairs well with mild or strong cheeses, salads, poultry, and barbecued and smoked meats.

- *Muscat Canelli* This sweet Italian wine is a natural at the dessert table, especially with desserts such as cheesecake.
- *Johannisberg Riesling* The Johannisberg Riesling wines range from dry to sweet and from light- to medium-bodied. Their fruitiness complements barbecued and smoked meats. The late harvest Rieslings are sweeter and are sometimes served as dessert wines.

 Red Wines

- *Pinot Noir* The major red wine of Burgundy, Pinot Noir is light- to medium-bodied. It pairs well with a variety of foods including salmon, tuna, poultry, pork, veal, beef, and lamb.
- *Cabernet Sauvignon* A Bordeaux-style wine, Cabernet Sauvignon is a medium- to full-bodied dry red wine that pairs well with red meats such as steaks and roasts, creamy fish dishes, pork, and veal. It is also sometimes served with chocolates.
- *Merlot* Merlot is a medium- to full-bodied dry red wine that is known for its mellowness. It pairs well with lighter meats (pork) and some game birds. Merlot can stand up to the strong flavors of roasted vegetables. However, if a dish is particularly garlicky, it will overpower the Merlot. This wine may also be paired with chocolates.
- *Sangiovese* The wine known for its use in Chianti, Sangiovese is light- to medium-bodied. It pairs well with Ital-

ian dishes such as lasagna, as well as grilled meats and vegetables.

 ## Champagne

With Champagnes made in Texas, there is even more reason to enjoy a bit of the bubbly at home. Dry Champagne is referred to as Brut, and it pairs well with chicken, shrimp, and fruit salads. Champagne literally adds a sparkling touch to a cocktail hour.

 Appendix E

Celebratory Dinners Featuring Texas Wines

Need a menu idea for a special dinner? Perhaps you will find inspiration in these menus, which were served to dignitaries from Texas and beyond. Each menu features a selection of Texas wines.

Reception Honoring Queen Elizabeth II—
May 21, 1991

Menu on Display at La Buena Vida Vineyards

Duck Confit Empanadas
Lobster Quesadillas with Mango Cream
Ceviche Tostadas with Black Beans
Southwestern Pizzettas
Garlic Shrimp with Smoked Tomatoes and Cilantro
Blue Corn Pancakes with Caviar and Red Pepper Crème
    Fraîche
Venison Chili Cups with Dallas Goat Cheese
Tropical Fruit Display with Texas Cheeses
Artesia Sparkling Water

Wines:

Texas Smith Estate Blanc de Blanc, Texas NL
Teysha Sauvignon Blanc, Texas 1990

Totally Texas Hunger's Feast—December 6, 1996, at the Texas Governor's Mansion

Menu on Display at Pheasant Ridge Winery

Texas Wild Boar and Tortilla Soup
Cilantro Glazed Pecan Smoked Quail on Garden Greens
Hill Country Axis Venison Stuffed with Gulf Prawns,
    served atop Medina Valley Apple Cider Glaze
Corn Pudding and Harvest Greens
Pumpkin Crème Brûlée

Wines:

1993 Pheasant Ridge Cabernet
1995 Llano Estacado Gewürztraminer
1994 Llano Estacado Chardonnay

The Sgarbossa Family Presents Friday Evening at Flat Creek Estate—June 7, 2002

Chef Silvia Sgarbossa brought the tastes of her restaurant in Veneto, Italy, to a Friday evening dinner at Flat Creek Estate. She prepared two special weekend meals and presented a

cooking class at the winery. (The recipe for Pere al Travis Peak
Select Cabernet Sauvignon is featured in chapter 11.)

Menu Available at Flat Creek Estate

Appetizer:

> Prosecco Veneto
> Cristini Pate di Carote
> Salsa di Pomodoro

Antipasti:

> Insalata Fantasia con Formaggi
> Melone alla Giasi
> Tacchino Sfizioso
> Rotolini Prosciutto
> Frittatine Erbe Aromatiche
> Crostini Polenta con Tropea
> Diavolini

Primi Piatti:

> Risotto alle Fragole
> Tagliatelle al Cacao
> Tagliatelle agli Agrumi
> Sorbetto agli Agrumi

Secondi Piatti:

> Spezzatino Veneto alla Travis Peak
> Lonza alle Prugne

Contorni:

Palate in Tecia Verdure Grigliate

Dessert:

Crema Catalana
Pere al Cabernet Travis Peak '99
Dolce Frutta
Fregolotta
Caffe

 Appendix F

Texas Wine Websites

The Internet is overflowing with the wonderful world of wine. Use the following lists as a guide to Texas wineries, cheese and chocolate makers, and wine-related websites.

Texas Vineyards and Wineries

Alamosa Wine Cellars	www.alamosawinecellars.com
Becker Vineyards	www.beckervineyards.com
Bell Mountain Vineyards (and Oberhof)	www.bellmountainwine.com
Blue Mountain Vineyard	link through www.fortdavis.com
Cap*Rock Winery	www.caprockwinery.com
Chisholm Trail Winery	www.chisholmtrailwinery.com
Delaney Vineyards	www.delaneyvineyards.com
Driftwood Vineyards	www.driftwoodvineyards.com
Dry Comal Creek Vineyards	www.drycomalcreek.com
Fall Creek Vineyards	www.fcv.com
Flat Creek Estate	www.flatcreekestate.com
Grape Creek Vineyard	www.grapecreek.com
Haak Vineyards & Winery	www.haakwine.com
La Bodega Winery	www.texaswinetrails.com/ bodega.htm
La Buena Vida Vineyards	www.labuenavida.com

LightCatcher Winery	www.lightcatcher.com
Llano Estacado Winery	www.llanowine.com
McReynolds Wines	www.mcreynoldswines.com
Messina Hof Winery & Resort	www.messinahof.com
Pheasant Ridge Winery	www.pheasantridgewinery.com
Pillar Bluff Vineyards	www.pillarbluff.com
Pleasant Hill Winery	www.pleasanthillwinery.com
Sister Creek Vineyards	www.sistercreekvineyards.com
Spicewood Vineyards	www.spicewoodvineyards.com
Ste. Genevieve Wines	www.tourtexas.com/fortstockton/ftstockbus.html
Texas Hills Vineyard	www.texashillsvineyard.com
Wichita Falls Vineyards & Winery	www.wichitafallsvineyardandwinery.com
Woodrose Winery & Resort	www.woodrosewinery.com

 ## Texas Cheese and Chocolate Websites

Marotti Biscotti—www.mbiscotti.com

Mozzarella Company—www.mozzco.com

New York, Texas, Cheesecake Co.—www.nytxccc.com

Quintessential Chocolates—go to www.gourmetfoodmall.com and click on "Candy & Chocolate" link

Miscellaneous Texas Wine Sites

Grapevine, Texas (home of Grape
  Fest)—www.grapevinetexasusa.com
Personal Wine, Inc. (personalized wine
  bottles)—www.personalwine.com
Saveur Texas Hill Country Wine & Food
  Festival—www.texaswineandfood.org
Texas Department of Agriculture (information on food,
  wine, and other Texas products)—www.gotexan.org
Texas Wine and Grape Growers
  Association—www.twgga.org
Texas Wine Tours (Hill Country wine
  tours)—www.texaswinetours.com
Texas Wine Trails (packed with information on Texas
  wines and wineries)—www.texaswinetrails.com
Wine Society of Texas—www.winesocietyoftexas.org

$Recipe\ Index$

(Name of winery or chef is in parentheses unless it is included in the recipe name.)

Fish

Pasta

 ## Pecans

 ## Pies and Tarts

 ## Pork

 ## Rabbit

 ## Sangria

 ## Seafood